PARADISE OF EXILES

PARADISE OF EXILES

The Anglo-American Gardens of Florence

KATIE CAMPBELL

FRANCES LINCOLN LIMITED
PUBLISHERS
www.franceslincoln.com

Frances Lincoln Limited
4 Torriano Mews
Torriano Avenue
London NW5 2RZ
www.franceslincoln.com

Printed in China

9 8 7 6 5 4 3 2 1

Commissioned and edited by Jane Crawley
Designed by Ian Hunt

HALF TITLE Mary Berenson in her garden at I Tatti

TITLE PAGE On the terrace at Villa Gamberaia

AUTHOR'S ACKNOWLEDGEMENTS

I would like to acknowledge my thesis supervisor, Dr Timothy Mowl, for his
unstinting support and Bristol University and the AHRC for financing the
research towards the PhD on which this book is based. I would also like to
thank Dr Jonathan Nelson from Syracuse University, Florence, Benedetta
Origo from La Foce, Federica Parretti from Villa Il Palmerino, Contessa
Lucrezia Fulcis from Villa Maiano, Allen Grieco from I Tatti and Giorgio
Galletti for advice and information.

CONTENTS

INTRODUCTION

'We slope to Italy at last/and youth, by green degrees.'
ROBERT BROWNING, By the Fireside

IN THE FINAL DECADES of the nineteenth century, Florence attracted an intriguing colony of English and American expatriates. Drawn by the faint glow of the Renaissance, these romantic adventurers bought up the crumbling villas abandoned during Italy's long struggle for unification. Restoring their noble dwellings, these latter-day Medici lived out the rural *otium* – the country life of ease described by Pliny in the first century AD. Some cast their lives as Virgilian idylls, combining modern farming techniques with classical wisdom to rescue the agricultural landscape from decades of neglect. Others explored local culture to produce a rich stream of novels, histories, essays, biographies, guidebooks and even a cookbook celebrating villa life. Still others pursued lives of leisure, cultivating themselves against the picturesque background of the Tuscan hills.

Among the more colourful characters of the community were the American art historian Bernard Berenson, a Faustian figure about whom it was said he could have been God but he chose instead to be Mephistopheles; the 'cad' Sir Arthur Acton and his fabulously wealthy American wife; the bereaved philosopher Charles Strong, whose Rockefeller in-laws financed his villa retreat; the cross-dressing English essayist Violet Paget, known to the world as Vernon Lee; the beautiful Romanian Princess Jeanne Ghika, who lived in seclusion with her American companion Miss Blood; the widowed Lady Sybil Cutting, who fled to Florence to evade her American in-laws; her daughter, the writer, Iris Origo; the eccentric English romance writer known as Ouida; the much-married American heiress Mabel Dodge Luhan, and the misanthropic aristocrat Sir George Sitwell.

Though art and history formed the main interests of the community, horticulture was a close second. The Anglo-Florentines injected new life into Tuscany's decrepit gardens; some attempted to recreate authentic Italian designs, touring the countryside for inspiration, trawling old libraries for treatises and manuals; others produced an anglicised version of the Italian style, smothering walls with scented climbers, replacing gravel terraces with emerald lawns, stuffing box parterres with bright bedding plants and filling their ancient orchards with exotic shrubs.

In his 1881 novel *The Portrait of a Lady,* Henry James' protagonist is seduced by her lover's Tuscan villa: 'antique, solid, weather-worn…hazy with Italian colour. It had a narrow garden, in the manner of a terrace, productive chiefly of tangles of wild roses and old stone benches, mossy and sun-warmed.' In his 1907 guidebook, *Italian Gardens*, George Elgood posits the ideal villa: 'the parterre spread out beneath the windows…shady places near at hand; fountains with plentiful water supply; and beyond the garden, away towards the hilly background, wild woodland stretches'. In her 1970 autobiography *Images and Shadows* Iris Origo describes her youthful desire for a fifteenth-century villa at the end of a long cypress avenue 'with an austere façade broken only by a deep loggia…a little courtyard with a well, and a garden with a fountain and an overgrown hedge of box'. These three descriptions, spread across several generations, reveal the consistency of the Anglo-Florentine villa fantasy. For almost a hundred years, from the unification of Italy till the outbreak of the Second World War, the image prevailed. It is this idea of villa life, the community which subscribed to it, and the gardens they created, that this book will explore.

OPPOSITE *George Elgood,* Florence from the Terrace of Il Palmieri *(detail), c.1900. One of England's finest watercolourists, Elgood (1851–1943) specialised in old gardens. He first discovered Italy in 1881 and returned annually thereafter, publishing* Italian Gardens *in 1907.*

ANGLOPHONES IN PARADISE

'What a tranquil, contented life it seemed, with romantic beauty as part of its daily texture! – the sunny terrace, with its tangled podere beneath it; the bright grey olives against the bright blue sky; the long, serene, horizontal lines of other villas, flanked by their upward cypresses, disposed upon the neighbouring hills; the richest little city in the world in a softly-scooped hollow at one's feet, and beyond it the most appealing of views, the most majestic, yet the most familiar.'

HENRY JAMES, Italian Hours

IN 1820 WHEN PERCY BYSSHE SHELLEY INVITED HIS COUSIN to join him in Florence, he described his adopted city as 'the paradise of exiles, the retreat of pariahs'. To many the Italian peninsula was associated with liberality – Napoleon having refused to criminalise homosexuality during his brief tenure as Emperor of Italy. Nonetheless not all the city's expatriates were sexual outcasts or social misfits. The English had been welcomed in Florence since the Middle Ages when British mercenaries were often employed to defend the city. Through the seventeenth and eighteenth centuries such travellers as John Milton and James Boswell wrote enthusiastically about the city, its neatness and industry being less threatening to northerners than the abject poverty and overt Catholicism of Rome and Naples to the south. But it was not until 1815, with the end of the Napoleonic Wars, that anglophone travellers began to arrive en masse.

Some were tourists, delighted to travel again after the decades of conflict that had kept them from the continent. Others came to settle, enchanted by the romance and the history, the climate and the culture of this outermost outpost of the civilised world. The development of the steam train in the 1850s meant travellers could reach Florence from London in thirty-six hours, where previously it had taken several weeks – a journey-time not altered since the days of the Roman Empire. Similarly the steamship brought the Old World within the reach of many Americans; by the middle of the nineteenth century a dozen ships a day were leaving New York City for Europe, provoking Henry James to complain that such 'perpetual ferryings' robbed travel of its romance.

As anglophones are notoriously wary of other languages, a whole network arose to service them in English: there were British pharmacists, American doctors, English speaking chemists, banks and grocery shops, Protestant churches and even an 'English' cemetery. Molini's stocked Reeves paints, pens and ink. Doney's Café in the fashionable Via Tornabuoni served muffins and seedcake for its anglophone clients. Dr Broomback's Academy, a mere twenty minutes walk from the Pitti Palace, catered for 'the Sons of Gentlemen', while the aptly named Old England provided everything from Oxford marmalade to tartan rugs. Vieusseux's Circulating Library offered English books and magazines. There were even several English language newspapers – the *Athenaeum*, the *Florence Herald* and the *Florence Directory* – duly recording the arrivals and departures of visitors as well as the social engagements of expatriate residents.

In 1853 the American journalist George Hilliard observed of the city's foreign community that the largest portion came from England, 'that country which is loved by its people with such pugnacious patriotism while they are always running away from its taxes, its dull climate, its sea-coal fires and the grim exclusiveness of its society.' Two years later the Goncourt brothers described Florence as '*Ville toute Anglaise',* where 'the palaces are almost the same dismal black as the city of London and where everything seems to smile upon the English'. Clearly the brothers did not distinguish between anglophone nations as already Americans made up a substantial portion of the expatriate population. By 1869, 30,000 of Florence's 200,000 inhabitants were British or American and by 1900 anglophones represented one sixth of the resident population, creating what the American writer Constance Fenimore Woolson dubbed 'that band of pilgrims from the land of fog and the land of haste who, having once fallen under the spell of Italy…return thither again and yet again'.

OPPOSITE *Biagio di Antonio,* Annunciation *(detail), c.1490 (Accademia Nazionale di San Luca, Rome). Florentine painters often featured the Tuscan countryside. Here the Villa Medici presides from its hilltop in Fiesole, a village much admired by the Anglo-Florentines, not least for its Etruscan origins.*

ABOVE *Lady Paget's medieval tower rising from the hilltop village of Bellosguardo. While Italians carefully gutted their ancestral dwellings to ensure hygiene and comfort, the Anglo-Florentines endured any amount of discomfort to preserve the air of romance and drama exuded by their venerable villas.*

Among these pilgrims, many, of both sexes, were fleeing family responsibilities, gender stereotypes and social ostracisation. Others were simply avoiding the humiliations of genteel poverty; those who could not afford an urban palazzo could rent rooms in the decaying dwellings of impecunious aristocrats. Still others were political idealists, fired by Italy's centuries-long battle for independence and unification.

In 1865 when the newly unified Italy chose Florence as its temporary capital, the city embarked on a frenzy of rebuilding. Medieval slums were cleared, ancient walls were demolished to create new housing districts and quaint back lanes were lost to the rational network of avenues without which no nineteenth-century metropolis could consider itself modern. Five years later when Rome was named the country's permanent capital, Florence sank into a stupor. Indigent and irrelevant, it attracted a new generation of foreigners looking for picturesque

accommodation, cheap staff and romantic settings. Decades of political turmoil had impoverished local aristocrats, forcing them to abandon their estates and sell off their possessions. The ensuing flood of art and antiquities attracted all manner of connoisseurs, collectors, scholars, dealers and con men.

While a few turned to the urban palazzi like their pre-unification forebears, most were drawn to the crumbling villas in the surrounding hills. Like the Medici before them, they fled the crowded city for the peace of the countryside, which unification had freed of revolutionaries for the first time in centuries. In 1878 Henry James complained, 'if you are an aching alien half the talk is about villas'; indeed those villas were so numerous that aching aliens could rent them, complete with tower, chapel and garden, for a mere 500 dollars a year. As James wryly observed, these noble dwellings had long outlived their original purpose: 'They weren't built with such a thickness of wall and depth of embrasure, such a solidity of staircase and superfluity of stone, simply to afford an economical winter residence to English and American families.' Yet it was English and American families which sought them out and gave them new life.

From such lofty hilltop havens, odd friendships flourished. To the south, beyond the Porta Romana, the young American Mabel Luhan befriended the ageing aristocrat Walburga, Lady Paget, who instructed her in the intricate, arcane and iron-clad rules of Florentine society. To the north, on the Montughi hill, dealer Sir Arthur Acton forged a useful alliance with the eccentric collector Sir Frederick Stibbert. Above them sat the hillside of Fiesole which Aldous Huxley disparaged as 'villadom'. Here, in the village of San Domenico, lived the scholar and essayist Vernon Lee, to whom the young art critic Bernard Berenson brought his first tentative letters of introduction. Also in San Domenico, the newcomer Joseph Lucas sought the advice of another formidable female essayist, Janet Ross. From her terrace down the hill Mary Berenson would signal to Ross each morning to confirm the day's engagements, while her husband forged a more intimate relationship with Lady Sybil Cutting, who lived in the venerable Villa Medici, Fiesole, just across from Berenson's Harvard friend Charles Strong at the Villa Le Balze.

Although Americans were less likely than their English counterparts to purchase estates and settle for life, many came for years at a time, renting grand apartments in even grander villas. American artists flocked to the city to view its master-pieces, copy its art works, study anatomy in its art classes and employ its accommodating nude models.

In 1870, when his Pre-Raphaelite style lost favour in America, Henry Roderick Newman (1843–1917) retreated to Florence, where, encouraged by John Ruskin, he embarked on a series of landscape studies which revived his artistic – and financial – fortunes. In 1903 the flamboyant Impressionist

William Merritt Chase (1849–1916) rented Villa La Meridiana near the Medici stronghold of Careggi; so delighted was he by the local colour that he returned each summer, eventually purchasing the Villa Silli south of the city where he created some of his most popular works.

In 1926 the eccentric painter Richard Blow purchased the unusual, polygonal Villa Marchi off the Piazza Calda and devoted himself to reviving the ancient Florentine craft of *intarsia* or *pietra dura* – creating images from intricately cut semi-precious stones. Having sought out the few remaining practitioners, Blow commissioned avant-garde artists like Giorgio de Chirico to produce modern designs which he promoted back home. While compositions depicting pistols and playing cards were popular in Texas, the American market generally preferred surrealist reclining nudes in desolate landscapes. Philosophical about his shift from artist to dealer, Blow remarked in a 1951 *Time* magazine interview: 'Intarsia may be a minor art, but hell, it's better to turn out a good piece of minor art than a bad piece of major art.'

American sculptors also flocked to Florence with its plentiful supply of marble and its ancient traditions of stone cutting and bronze casting. Hiram Powers (1805–73), the son of a Vermont farmer, was so inspired by his first visit that he settled in a house on the Via Fornace. Imitating his Renaissance forebears Powers specialised in idealised human forms, the most famous of which, *The Greek Slave*, depicts a naked woman bound in chains. A masterpiece of neoclassical kitsch, the work was promoted as an allegory of Christian forbearance before being taken up by the abolitionist movement and becoming the most popular art work in America. More than 100,000 people paid to see it when it toured the country in 1847, and four years later it was the centrepiece in London's Crystal Palace Exhibition. Powers himself went on to teach at the city's prestigious Accademia and was finally buried, along with several of his children, in the *Cemitero Protestante di Porta a' Pinti* – better known as the English Cemetery because, although it houses representatives of sixteen nations, more than half of its 1,400 graves are English or American.

American writers were also inspired by the city's literary and historic heritage. In his preface to *The Marble Faun* (1860), Nathaniel Hawthorne notes the difficulty of writing in his native land: 'there is no shadow, no antiquity, no mystery, no picturesque and gloomy wrong, nor anything but a commonplace prosperity, in broad and simple daylight'. Hailed by many as his greatest work, the novel depicts a group of naïve Americans encountering the pagan in Italy; while much of it is set in Rome, the story is based on characters Hawthorne met in the Anglo-Florentine community.

BELOW *Lizzie Boott Duveneck,* Villa Castellani, *1887. For many years the American artist rented apartments in this picturesque villa, first with her father, then with her husband.*

ABOVE *Thomas Hartley Cromeck,* View from Bellosguardo, c.1845. *Dramatic views of Florence from the surrounding hill towns were favoured by the Anglo-Florentines who liked to think of the city as timeless, eternal and unaltered since the early Renaissance.*

LEFT Cimitero Protestante di Porta a'Pinti. *Better known as the English Cemetery, this was the final resting place of many of the Anglo-Florentines. Enclosed in neo-classical walls, punctuated by smoky cypresses, shaded by dense hedges and billowing trees, it sits in splendid isolation, utterly detached from the cacophony of modern life which surges around it.*

In 1857 Hiram Powers rented the Hawthornes a thirteen room apartment in the Casa de Bello opposite his own house. Close to the open spaces of the Boboli gardens, the romantic cloisters of the Villa Annalena and the densely planted English-style parkland of the Villa Torrigiani, this idyllic spot delighted its tenants. Sophia Hawthorne recorded in her diary:

Florence is as enchanting as I expected. It is a place to live and be happy in – so cheerful, so full of art…the air is full of the songs of birds. The merlins are in choir over against our terrace, in a wood of the Torrigiani gardens, the marble busts on their pedestals seem to enjoy themselves in the bosky shade. The green lizards run across the parapet and to exist is a joy….Mr Hawthorne is luxuriating down in the garden, buried up in roses and jessamine.

Hawthorne himself wrote: 'I hardly think there can be a place in the world where life is more delicious for its own simple sake than here.'

Nonetheless, at the onset of summer the Hawthornes, like many of their compatriots, retreated from the heat of the city. In the hilltop village of Bellosguardo they found the Villa di Montauto. Though Hawthorne described it as 'big enough to quarter a regiment', they rented it from a local aristocrat for just twenty-eight dollars a month. Sophia extolled the garden, with its deeply shaded avenues, clear, smooth lawn and semicircular terraces. What most impressed both Hawthornes, however, was the stone tower at the end of the property – haunted by the ghost of its most famous prisoner, the reforming fifteenth-century friar, Giralamo Savonarola. Not surprisingly, this tower served as a key setting in *The Marble Faun,* while Bellosguardo

BELOW *For centuries tourists flocked to the Piazza della Signoria to gaze at Cellini's sensuous* Perseus, *Giambologna's muscular* Rape of the Sabine Women *and Michelangelo's monumental* David *(1504), whose depiction of the biblical shepherd/liberator symbolised the defence of civic liberties by the Florentine Republic; such celebrations of the naked male body attest to the city's famed tolerance and liberality.*

itself became a favourite retreat among the Anglo-Florentine community.

Another intriguing dwelling was the Villa Castellani – later known as the Villa Mercedes – a fortress-like building on the main square. Typically Tuscan, the villa has a long, blank façade and a low, overhanging roof that creates deep shadows to cool the interior. In the nineteenth century the villa was owned by an American family which let spacious apartments round the central courtyard to friends and acquaintances. In 1887 Constance Fenimore Woolson, rented part of the villa, which she describes in her short story *Dorothy* as 'an ancient structure of pale yellow hue…[tenanted] by people of English and American birth'.

One of these tenants was the newly-widowed painter Francis Boott, who quit his native Boston in the 1850s to seek solace in the Tuscan hills, settling in the villa with his young daughter Elizabeth. Lizzie, as she was always known, became an artist in her own right and braved paternal disapproval to marry her teacher, the charming, feckless Cincinnati painter, Frank Duveneck. After an initial *froideur*, the three settled in together and both villa and surrounding farmlands feature in their paintings of the period. The Bootts had befriended Henry James in 1865 when they returned to Boston for a prolonged visit at the end of the civil war; later, as a frequent visitor to their Italian apartments, James used the villa as his inspiration for the Villa Pandolfini in his first novel *Roderick Hudson*. Later, he reprised it as the elegant home of the sinister Gilbert Osmond in *The Portrait of a Lady*. Lizzie herself, although she was only three years James' junior, is reputed to be the model for the docile Pansy, Osmond's oppressed but dutiful daughter.

Another local dwelling much loved within the community was the Villa Brichieri-Colombi down the hill from the main square. James praised it as 'the centre of histories, memories, echoes, all generations deep'. In 1888 he succumbed to its charms and rented an apartment there in which he wrote

The Aspern Papers. Though set in Venice to disguise its source, the novel was based on the life of Byron's lover, Claire Clairmont, a local curiosity who lived out her days in Florence preserving her memories from inquisitive scholars.

As with many Tuscan villas, what Brichieri-Colombi lacked in formal gardens it more than made up for with spectacular views. Elizabeth Barrett Browning extolled the view in *Aurora Leigh* – that much-loved poem about a courageous woman who flees a stifling life in London, rejects conventional marriage to live by her pen and ends up in a hilltop villa with spectacular views overlooking Florence. Browning, like James, had been introduced to the villa while visiting Isabella Blagden (1818–73) who lived there from 1845 until her death nearly thirty years later. A prominent Anglo-Florentine writer in her day, Blagden is chiefly remembered for her romance with Edward Robert Bulwer-Lytton, 1st Earl of Lytton, who published poetry under the name of Owen Meredith and became – a rather brutal – Viceroy of India. When the taint of foreign blood prevented her from marrying her beloved, both parties exploited their misfortune and immortalised their tragedy, Blagden in her novel *Agnes Tremorne* and Lytton in his verse epic *Lucile*.

Another of Bellosguardo's intriguing residents was Mrs George Keppel, consort of King Edward VII and distant ancestor of Prince Charles' own Camilla Parker Bowles. Keppel arrived in Florence in 1924 seeking discreet retirement after the death of her protector and the chaos of the First World War. This she found in the Villa L'Ombrellino, named for the decorative nineteenth-century metal umbrella in its garden. Built in the fourteenth century, the villa was rented, for a time, by Galileo, whose two daughters resided in the nearby Convento di San Matteo. While his legitimate daughter was allowed to write to him, his illegitimate daughter was not. Nonetheless the nuns retained hope for his soul; in December 1625 Sister Maria Celeste sent Galileo several baked pears and a late blooming rose, explaining that the thorns recalled the Passion of Christ, the leaves suggested hope and the flower itself signified that the winter of this life would be followed by eternal spring in heaven.

In the early nineteenth century the Italian poet Ugo Foscolo composed his famous poem *Le Grazie* while a guest at the Villa

L'Ombrellino, and several decades later the American scholar Charles Eliot Norton lodged there during one of his many extended stays in the city. When Keppel arrived she replaced the Victorian palms with Venetian statues and smothered the garden wall with wisteria, whose purple fronds framed the view of Florence to the north. In typically English fashion Keppel stuffed great terracotta tubs with azaleas and gardenias – carefully over-wintered in the villa's hothouse. Further proclaiming her patrimony with a staggering lack of sympathy for local horticultural traditions, she commissioned the English designer Cecil Pinsent to transform the front terrace into a Union Jack garden, with bisecting paths in the form of the British flag. Happily, the garden is little more than a platform for the surrounding views, although Osbert Sitwell, a guest at the villa, noted that every morning his formidable hostess would walk with her gardener, exclaiming 'bisogna begonia' and stabbing the earth with her walking stick where she felt the flower beds needed embellishment.

Although Keppel herself was far too grand to fraternise with the Anglo-Florentines, her husband exhibited an unhealthy interest in the young women of the community whom he used to invite to ride in his red Lancia before proposing intimate photography sessions in his private studio. A generation later Keppel's daughter, Violet Trefusis, maintained the tradition of scandal by conducting a very public love affair with Vita Sackville-West. Like her mother, Violet eschewed the Anglo-Florentines, preferring her French chateau outside Paris. She did maintain the villa, however, and was particularly proud of the iris garden with its many hues of blue. In her

BELOW *George Elgood,* Azaleas, *1904. Although Edith Wharton deplored their addiction to 'flower-loveliness', the Anglo-Florentines supplemented the austere evergreens and classical stonework of traditional Italian horticulture with bursts of colour, often derived from potted plants which could be removed when they faded under the desiccating summer sun.*

ABOVE *The Sage of Settignano and the Last Aesthete in the early 1950s. After the Second World War Bernard Berenson and Harold Acton stayed on at their villas promoting the memory and preserving the values of the Anglo-Florentine community.*

autobiographical *Prelude to Misadventure*, Trefusis reveals that she was not immune to L'Ombrellino's dramatic views, extolling 'the predatory, hawklike silhouette of the Palazzo Vecchio, the sprawled, beautifully composed town, which hung back from the Arno's nonchalant escape into the greenest of pastoral landscapes', adding, 'everywhere the punctuation of cypresses, with here and there a stab of purple bougainvillea, gave the right value to church and campanile.'

An equally intriguing local resident was the novelist known as Ouida whose pseudonym is a childhood mispronounciation of her Christian name. In 1871 Louisa de la Ramée retreated from the furore following her publication of several sensational romance novels. Quitting her native Bury St Edmunds she rented the Villa Farinola, high up on a mountainside at Scandicci just south of Bellosguardo. Ouida used the villa as a template in her 1873 novel *Pascarel*, describing it as, 'vast dusky, crumbling, desolate without, as all such places are, and within full of that harmless charm of freedom, space, antiquity, and stillness that does no less perpetually belong to them'.

In a community of eccentrics, Ouida reigned supreme, renowned, among other things, for allowing her dogs to eat at table off priceless china and relieve themselves where they chose. She could write a story worth £200 in three days, and although she was paid handsomely for each of her many novels,

she spent the money as fast as she made it, driving around in silk-lined carriages, hosting literary salons, dressing in hugely expensive Worth gowns and pursuing grotesque passions for unsuitable younger men. Believing plants, like dogs, should be given free rein, Ouida refused to maintain her garden till eventually her landlord evicted her for negligence. Moving to Viareggio, she replaced human with canine companions, and although her novels proclaim the nobility of the Tuscan peasant, she ended her days impoverished, emaciated, persecuted by the local people and shunned by her own community. While she proclaimed herself the greatest author ever, what really alienated her fellow Anglo-Florentines were her *romans à clef*, particularly the ill-named *Friendship* which depicted the community as a seething stew of arrogant, competitive, talentless charlatans.

Across the city in the northern hilltown of Settignano sense prevailed over sensuality. Here the American writer Mark Twain claimed he had written more in four months than he could in two years at home. In his autobiography he celebrated the view from the Villa Viviani which he rented in 1892, claiming, 'After nine months of familiarity with this panorama I still think, as I thought in the beginning, that this is the fairest picture on our planet, the most enchanting to look upon, the most satisfying to the eye and the spirit.'

Buoyed by such revivifying views, the Anglo-Florentines pursued their charmed lives. Undaunted by the pandemonium of the First World War or the inter-war rise of fascism, they continued cultivating their gardens, writing their books, acquiring art and entertaining the well read and the well bred through the turmoil of the 1920s. It was not until the eve of the Second World War that the idyll finally ended when Italy joined the Axis side against the Allies. Overnight English and American residents found themselves enemy aliens. Reluctantly

ABOVE *Sir George Sitwell entertaining Crown Prince Rupert of Bavaria in the Cardinal's Garden at Montegufoni.*

they dispersed, returning to homelands which were no longer home. Many of them died during the war, others were too old to resume their earlier lives amid post-war privations, still others had not the heart to restore their war-damaged properties.

At this point many of the Anglo-Florentine villas were sold to affluent Italians, turned into hotels or bequeathed to academic institutions. Two members of the community however, Bernard Berenson and Harold Acton, having nowhere else to go, simply returned to their villas. Living relics of the past, they became key features in any cultural tour of the city.

During the early post-war years anglophone interest in Italy waned, not least because of the taint of fascism attached to its past and the fear of communism lurking in its future. A few affluent eccentrics, however, continued to live the Anglo-Florentine fantasy; after an indiscretion involving call girls and other intoxicants the late Lord Lambton retired to Tuscany to restore his Villa Cetinale. At about the same time an American

novelist Paul Gervais and his partner Gil Cohen stumbled across the Villa Massei, a crumbling renaissance hunting lodge. Like their predecessors they renovated the estate, created a magnificent garden and duly recorded their experience. Gervais' *A Garden in Lucca: Finding Paradise in Tuscany*, follows the well-established precedent, combining wit, gossip, horticulture, ancient history and local lore to create an erudite and entertaining read.

Recently the Tuscan countryside has been colonised by a new generation of Anglo-Florentines. Less affluent than their forebears, they have eschewed the grand villas, looking instead to the farmhouses and outbuildings abandoned after the Second World War when Italians left the land to pursue less arduous jobs in cities and towns. Although different in scale, this modern iteration of the Anglo-Florentine idyll demonstrates the enduring power of that dream of villa life first promoted by English and American expatriates more than a century ago.

LEFT *The Villa Cetinale was famous for its Scala Santa rising steeply through the grounds to a hilltop hermitage. Built on Etruscan foundations the villa began as a modest farmhouse; it was expanded in the Baroque style by Cardinal Fabio Chigi before he became Pope Alexander VII in 1655. In the 1970s Lord Lambton purchased the estate and in true Anglo-Florentine fashion restored the villa and created an elegant Italianate garden.*

VILLA LIFE AND THE IDEA OF FLORENCE

*'My beautiful Florence! The flower of cities,
the most highly cultivated of communities, the very rose of civilization.'*
NATHANIEL HAWTHORNE

WHILE THE ANCIENT ROMANS used their villas as a respite from public office and the Renaissance merchants saw the villa as an antidote to urban commerce, for the Anglo-Florentines villa life represented an escape from the modern world. Henry James spoke of the city's 'many-memoried streets', while Mabel Luhan observed, 'everyone played with the past in Florence. It was the material of their day.' As the birthplace of the Renaissance, Florence was credited with inventing both capitalism and republicanism. Even more powerful for the Anglo-Florentines, however, was the legacy of its earlier inhabitants, the Etruscans.

Thought to be the most ancient and civilised of Italy's indigenous tribes, the Etruscans provided an early image of Italian nationhood. In the sixth century BC their lands, known as Etruria, extended from the Po valley in the north to the Bay of Naples in the south. By the nineteenth century nothing remained except a few painted tombs and some inscriptions, nonetheless the Anglo-Florentines eulogised the long-vanquished empire, filling their letters, essays and fiction with Etruscan references. In Byron's poem *Childe Harold*, Florence is lauded as 'the Etrurian Athens'. Lady Paget's diaries enthuse over Cornato's Etruscan necropolis, while the protagonists in William Dean Howells' *Indian Summer* extol Fiesole's Etruscan wall, whose huge blocks of stone lie as evenly 'as if placed there a year ago'. Even the controversial D.H.Lawrence spent his final days conjuring Etruria; his posthumously published *Etruscan Places* (1932) imagines a joyful, natural civilisation, in stark contrast to his own soulless, modern, industrial world. Although clearly

a dying man's fantasy of a life-affirming culture, the book's instant success reveals the potency of the Etruscan myth.

While Etruria may have represented life and liberty to the Anglo-Florentines, in the fourth century BC the region was conquered by the Romans. By 59 BC, Julius Caesar had established the colony of Florentia, setting aside the fertile valley for retired army veterans. Though the colony was, in fact, named after a Roman general, the Anglo-Florentines persisted in referring to it as 'the city of flowers'. With its lush surroundings and the waters of the Arno providing easy access to sea ports, Florentia flourished.

About this time Roman expansion began to change agricultural practice. As grain could be imported cheaply from colonies in North Africa, Roman farmers started concentrating on olives and grapes, shaping the landscape into the patchwork of vineyards and groves celebrated in classical literature. Gradually small farms were absorbed into larger estates creating a new class of farmer which had little contact with the land. With their estates overseen by managers and worked by slaves or labourers, these wealthy landowners began to use their country villas for relaxation rather than toil.

One of the earliest Latin texts to survive is Cato's *De Agricultura* (c.160 BC), an essay on rural life which provides practical advice on the managing of commercial farms. By the first century AD the villa had evolved from simple agricultural estate to suburban pleasure ground incorporating aviaries, ornamental fish ponds and exotic beasts. In his famous *Letters*, Pliny the Younger (c.61–115) advocates the restorative *otium*, or leisure, of a rural sojourn as an antidote to the *negotium*, or business, of city life. Thus the concept of the *villeggiatura*, the rural retreat, was born.

Although many Latin writers wrote lyrically about rural life, the one most revered by the Anglo-Florentines was Publius Virgilius Maro, otherwise known as Virgil (70–19 BC). His four-part pastoral *Georgics* was a staple of the English education,

OPPOSITE *Benozzo Gozzoli,* Procession of the Magi *(detail), 1459 (Chapel of the Magi, Palazzo Medici-Riccardi, Florence). Gozzoli set his procession in the Florentine countryside with his Medici patrons as the wise men. His training as a goldsmith explains the extraordinary detail and precision which have made these frescoes invaluable for historians of Renaissance architecture, horticulture, landscape and costumes.*

LEFT *Farming techniques had changed very little since classical times; Janet Ross asserted that the best commentary on Virgil's* Georgics *was the agricultural practice of her own peasant farmers. As this family photo shows, the harvest was conducted with ancient wooden ox-carts.*

Virgil provided a romantic precedent for Anglo-Florentine villa life. Few in the community could resist a classical allusion, and those who worked the land were particularly conscious of their illustrious forebears. Janet Ross proudly asserted that the best commentary on the *Georgics* was modern Tuscan farming; she trained her own vines through pear trees as Virgil recommended and was delighted to discover that the beehives of her tenants were made of hollowed willow trunks just as he had described his own. Similarly, for Joseph Lucas, even the most modest vineyard conjured visions of Arcadia, while Iris Origo proudly recounts that the rogation rites practised by her parish priest were similar to those recorded by Virgil nearly 2,000 years before.

As the rural idyll depicted by classical writers depended on peace and prosperity, the *villeggiatura* began to disappear in the fourth century when barbarians from the north began overrunning the countryside. Many villas were fortified, becoming the castles and monasteries which dot the Italian hilltops today; others were simply abandoned as people retreated to the safety of walled cities leaving their fields to revert to forests which soon filled with savage beasts and bandits.

Florence itself fell in the sixth century when it was taken by the 'long-beards' or Lombards during the invasions which marked the end of the Roman Empire. Eventually absorbed into the Holy Roman Empire, Florence was ruled by imperial margraves, the last of whom, Countess Matilda, set the region on its way to greatness once again. After her abduction by the German emperor, Matilda switched her allegiance to the papacy in the protracted disputes between emperor – represented by the Ghibellines – and pope – represented by the Guelphs. On her death in 1115 Florence became a commune, enabling it to pursue its republican and capitalist destiny.

The newly independent city was governed by an elected council of one hundred men known as the *signoria* after the turreted Florentine palace from whence they presided. Led by the *gonfaloniere*, the *signoria* consisted of eight executives, six of whom came from the powerful guilds of bankers, merchants and lawyers, while only two came from the more numerous but less influential guilds of shopkeepers and craftsmen. Despite this lack of true representation, in an era of absolute rulers Florence provided an image of popular power which remained potent into the nineteenth century when Elizabeth Barrett Browning decorated her salon green, red and white in honour of the – then illegal – Florentine flag.

Although change is always slower in rural areas, with the rise of individual rights in the thirteenth century, medieval serfdom was abolished in favour of the *mezzadria*, a system of sharecropping where tenants worked the landlord's estate for a percentage of the harvest. A century later the bubonic plague which ravaged Europe drove many people out of the cities and back to the countryside. Decimating a third of the population, the pestilence ensured social mobility for survivors; it also caused a religious crisis which undermined the power of the Church. These shifts in religious and social attitudes, plus improvements in travel and trade, helped give rise to a powerful merchant class.

Meanwhile, the crusades of the twelfth century, plus the thirteenth-century conquest of Moorish Spain, had unearthed the ancient texts preserved in Islamic libraries. The recovery of ancient science, maths, medicine and astrology encouraged scholars to turn from Christian faith to classical reason. Cut off from the prescriptive rule of Rome and free of the orthodoxy of the universities, Florence was the first city to exploit this rediscovered knowledge. Adopting pagan symbolism and celebrating the natural world, the Florentines initiated the movement which became known as humanism.

With its republican government, flourishing guilds and strong economy based on banking and textiles, fourteenth-century Florence became the richest city in Europe, despite the ongoing battle between emperor and pope. Ironically these tumultuous years gave rise to Italy's greatest writers – Dante (1265–1321), Petrarch (1304–74) and Boccaccio (1313–75). Indeed, on quitting Cincinnati for Florence, the nineteenth-century novelist Frances Trollope describes how she felt she was about to 'enter bodily into the presence of Dante, Petrarch and Boccaccio'.

Of the three, Dante was perhaps the most appealing to the Anglo-Florentines. Known as 'the great fugitive', he was banished in 1302 in an internal dispute between Guelph factions and when he was not composing his Divine Comedy he spent much of his life writing lyrically about his lost homeland. Petrarch, a diplomat and scholar, traversed the peninsula seeking ancient texts and promoting classical knowledge; he is credited with inventing the concept of 'the dark ages' between the classical world of ancient Rome and the Renaissance rediscovery of that world. This concept was particularly attractive to the Anglo-Florentines, who saw themselves as recovering the lost culture of the Renaissance.

Petrarch's friend Boccaccio is best known for his book the *Decameron*. Often hailed as the first ever novel, this collection of tales within tales describes the rural idyll of a group of youths who leave Florence to escape the 1348 plague. With its celebration of Tuscan rural life, the *Decameron* provided a template for the Anglo-Florentines, several of whom claimed their villas featured in the novel. A more muscular link with the

BELOW *Virgil's* Georgics, *c.1450, attributed to Apollonio di Giovanni (Biblioteca Riccardiana, Florence). This illuminated manuscript depicts the timeless agricultural techniques that were still used in late-nineteenth-century Tuscany.*

fourteenth century was English mercenary John Hawkwood (d.1394), whom the community celebrated as the first Anglo-Florentine, overlooking the fact that for much of his career Hawkwood fought with the Pisans against Florence.

Although the city remained, theoretically, a republic, it reached its cultural apex under the benign control of a single family. In 1434 Cosimo de' Medici (1389–1468) – known as Cosimo the Elder – packed the *signoria* with supporters to become the unofficial ruler of Florence. His firm but enlightened leadership initiated a period of stability, prosperity and artistic excellence which climaxed under his grandson, Lorenzo the Magnificent (1449–92), of whom the sixteenth-century historian Lodovici Guicciardini later observed: 'Florence could not have had a better or more delightful tyrant.'

Although the family's decline began with Lorenzo's death, the Medici continued to dominate for three centuries, consolidating control of Tuscany and reviving the glory of ancient Etruria. In 1494 the Medici were exiled at the behest of the puritanical Dominican priest Savonarola – whose 'bonfires of the vanities' consumed many of the city's artistic masterpieces. The family was reinstated, then ousted several more times before establishing itself among the great European dynasties. In 1532 Alessandro de' Medici was proclaimed the first Duke of Florence. Five years later, on his assassination, his role was taken by Lorenzo's great-nephew Cosimo I. By aligning with the French king, Cosimo had himself crowned Grand Duke of Tuscany then secured the family's position by marrying his eldest son, Francesco, to Joan of Austria, sister of the Habsburg emperor.

As early as the mid-fifteenth century, however, the Medici were already Europe's most successful bankers, investing in loans, currency exchange, commodities and insurance, trading

with the Ottomans, acting as royal bankers and collecting taxes for the Catholic Church. They also diversified, exploiting the land itself through mining, farming and porcelain factories, repopulating the countryside which had been largely abandoned since the fall of the Roman Empire. Integral with this process was the development of rural real estate; then, as now, property was seen as a safe, long-term investment and merchant families were quick to buy up land outside the cities.

It is at this point that the concept of the *villeggiatura* was revived, in part, because the expanding population made urban life, especially in the heat of summer, virtually unbearable. The air in Florence was particularly putrid as the surrounding hills prevented breezes from circulating, while the city's wool-dyeing industry depended on human urine, which, once used, was dumped with the rest of the raw sewage into open ditches. Spurred by commercial incentive, drawn to the rural lifestyle, inspired by the example of the ancients, Florence's mercantile leaders established a web of villas around the city. Not surprisingly, the Medici provided the template for the new villas.

At the time, the architect Leon Battista Alberti (1404–72), often described as the father of humanism, began promoting the ideas of the ancients in his *De Re Aedificatoria,* or *Ten Books on Architecture.* Though primarily concerned with architecture, the treatise, which was published, posthumously, in 1485, has a section on villas which discusses the layout and ornamentation of gardens. Here Alberti reintroduced the idea of grottoes and topiary, and advocated the use of statuary in the garden. He also recommended hilltop sites to ensure cooling breezes and commanding views of farmland, plains and distant cities. More practically, he advised that villas should encompass fields to supply grain, woods to support game and streams to provide fresh water and fish. Not surprisingly, such covetable sites matched the portfolio of his Medici patrons whose fortified farms and hunting lodges were being transformed into humanist villas.

At Il Trebbio, Cafaggiolo and Careggi, Cosimo's favourite architect, Michelozzo Michelozzi (1396–1472), pierced defensive walls with windows and transformed ramparts into airy loggias. Despite this innovative pursuit of lightness and grace, the early Medici villas retained a medieval bulk and drama which was much loved by the early Anglo-Florentines five centuries later. Janet Ross' ancient fortress Poggio Gherardo, John

BELOW *Martyrdom of Savonarola in the Piazza dell Signoria, c.1498, anon. (Museo San Marco, Florence). In 1497 Savanarola convinced many Florentines to burn their luxuries in a central Bonfire of the Vanities; the following year the mood shifted and he was burned as a heretic on the same spot.*

Temple Leader's castle Vincigliata and Lady Paget's turreted Bellosguardo all exude a heavy, austere gravity which their owners steadfastly refused to soften. Sir George Sitwell even emphasised the medieval atmosphere of his Montegufoni by embellishing the courtyard with a pyramid of cannonballs.

Even the innovative Villa Medici, Fiesole, which Michelozzi designed from scratch, retains a medieval mass. Nonetheless, this dwelling, conceived to express the new humanist celebration of nature, pioneered a new approach by replacing the central courtyard with a grand salon linked to the countryside beyond with loggias at both ends. With this innovation Michelozzi transformed the Florentine villa from an inward-looking fortress, to an outward looking retreat.

After Cosimo the Elder died in 1464, his grandson, Lorenzo, introduced new elegance to the rural villa. At Poggio

ABOVE *With its clear typeface, elegant layout and stylish woodcuts the mysterious 1499* Hypnerotomachia Poliphili *was enormously influential in promoting antique design in Renaissance Europe. Although variously attributed to Alberti and Lorenzo the Magnificent, an acrostic formed by each chapter's elaborately embellished first letter attributes the book to Francesco Colonna.*

a Caiano Lorenzo instructed his architect, Giuliano da Sangallo (1445–1516), to convert the medieval hunting lodge into a comfortable retreat. While Sangallo copied Michelozzi in replacing the central courtyard with a magnificent salon, he established a new relationship between the villa and its surroundings by raising the *piano nobile* onto an arcaded terrace. While this protected the villa from the flooding of the nearby river, ensured cool summer breezes and provided spectacular views of the surrounding countryside, it also raised the living space above the land, suggesting supremacy rather than integration.

Sangallo then linked interior to exterior with a temple-like portico whose origins in sacred Greek architecture proclaimed his patron's classical allegiances. Despite their innovations in finance and trade, the Medici carefully aligned themselves with the past in matters of philosophy and design; as Giorgio Vasari later explained in his *Ragionamenti*: 'because the antiquity of things of the past casts more honour, greatness and admiration on its relics than do modern things'. But there was something more at work than mere allusion to the past. This temple-like portico with its distinct triangular pediment had been adopted by Roman emperors to assert the divine authority of their power. By using this motif for a secular dwelling, Sangallo appears to be conferring similar status on his patron.

The publication, in 1499, of *Hypnerotomachia Poliphili* – a mysterious text believed to have been written by the Dominican monk, Francesco Colonna – further promoted the growing interest in antiquity. Although presented as a Christian allegory, this esoteric work idealised the pagan culture of the past. Its several hundred woodcuts depict intricate topiary, parterres, garden structures, grottoes, niches, statuary and elaborate waterworks. Written in the vulgar Italian of the time, *Hypnerotomachia* was one of the first books to be reproduced by the recently developed printing press. Its influence was profound, not least because it inspired a vogue for topiary – an art form which had delighted the ancient Romans with its melding of nature and art. Where Pliny recorded whole names and bestiaries carved in box, his Renaissance imitators confined themselves to simple walls and geometric forms. Also copying the ancients, Renaissance garden makers created *nymphaea* and groves to evoke the water nymphs and woodland dryads of classical antiquity.

Despite such embellishments, Tuscany's rocky topography militated against the sprawling gardens of the Veneto to the north, while an absence of water prevented the elaborate cascades of the villas D'Este, Lante and Farnese to the south. Indeed, throughout its history the Tuscan garden retained a sober, human scale, never straying far from the medieval *hortus conclusus* – that utilitarian enclosure of medicinal herbs, flowers and fruit.

In the mid-sixteenth century the architect Bernardo Buontalenti (1536–1608) ushered in the exuberant new style known as Baroque. Having served as military engineer for the Grand Dukes Francesco 1 (1541–87) and Ferdinand 1 (1549–1609), Buontalenti renovated the Medici villas of La Magia, Pratolino, La Petraia, Artimino, Ambrogiana and Lappeggi, transforming them from humanist retreats into sumptuous royal courts. While retaining the massive rusticated ground floors, he added luxurious salons and embellished the gardens using military hydraulic techniques to create elaborate fountains and amusing automata.

This lively style was favoured by the majority of Anglo-Florentines, not least because most of their villas had been built in the baroque era. Origo's La Foce, Luhan's Villa Curonia, Acton's La Pietra, the Crawfords' Il Palmieri, Lady Scott's Villa Capponi and even Berenson's I Tatti exhibit the thrusting balconies, balustrades, cornices, cartouches, pediments and pilasters which epitomise this exuberant style.

At its apex in the sixteenth century, the Florentine villa garden sparked many imitators, but the decline set in almost immediately. By the seventeenth century Florentine gardens were adopting elements of the French style, replacing simple geometry with elaborate 'embroidery' parterres, supplanting the limited palette of evergreens with deciduous trees and lurid exotics from the New World and the Far East. The waning of the Medici fortunes meant the mantle of horticultural innovation passed from Florence to Rome, where, in the absence of a local aristocracy or a newly-rich merchant class, cardinals and popes competed to display their power and wealth through extended parks and elaborate gardens.

In 1737 the last Medici died without heir and Tuscany passed to the Habsburg Empire. One particularly enlightened grand duke, Pietro Leopoldo (1765–90), astounded all Europe with his civil, criminal and ecclesiastical reforms. A century after Leopold abolished capital punishment, W.D.Howells shrewdly observed, 'Leopold found that the abolition of the death penalty resulted not in more, but in fewer crimes of

violence; yet the law continues to kill murderers, even in Massachusetts.' Though Massachusetts has since abolished the death penalty, over half of America's states have yet to reach the enlightened condition of eighteenth-century Florence.

One of Leopold's boldest innovations was freedom of worship; while designed to entice Protestant and Jewish craftsmen and merchants to the region, it succeeded in attracting all manner of libertines, among them, Charles Edward Louis Philip Casimir Stuart. After failing to secure the English throne in the 1746 Jacobite Uprising, 'Bonnie Prince Charlie' retreated to Florence, settling in a palazzo beneath a weathervane emblazoned CR – for *Carolus Rex*. In that unhappy villa, the only property owned by the Stuarts in more than a century of exile, the Young Pretender drank himself to death, providing fodder for generations of biographers. Equally appealing was his beautiful young wife who eloped from her abusive husband

with the Italian dramatist, Count Vittorio Alfieri. The couple's residence, the Casa Alfieri, later housed the British Consulate to the delight of those who renewed their visas in rooms once inhabited by the woman known variously as the Queen of England, the Queen of Florence, and, no doubt, the Queen of Hearts.

In 1796 Napoleon invaded the peninsula and later declared himself Emperor of France and King of Italy. Although his forced abdication in 1814 returned the Grand Duchy to the Habsburgs, Napoleon's brief reign fuelled the long-held desire for unification. Through the nineteenth century the various states, duchies and dynasties that made up the Italian peninsula gradually united. During the conflict many aristocrats abandoned their undefended rural estates; those who remained tended to follow the taste for the *giardino inglese*, replacing expensive formal gardens with naturalistic parks. In 1860 Tuscany joined the United Kingdom of Italy; in 1865 Florence was named the temporary capital and five years later when Rome joined the union, the unification process was complete.

LEFT *Pagan caryatids at Poggio a Caiano demonstrate Lorenzo's fascination with the classical past.*

ABOVE *The austere building behind Gamberaia's baroque* limonaia *is believed to be the original villa on the estate. Eberlein recounts a Tuscan superstition that the devil can only enter rooms that are absolutely symmetrical, to this he attributes the 'amazing inequalities' he encountered while measuring such early villas.*

It was at this point that the Tuscan villa was discovered by the Anglo-Florentines. As Edith Wharton explained, the country houses were often more splendid than any urban palace, and they were so densely set among the olive orchards and vineyards that 'the traveller thought himself in Florence three leagues before reaching the city'. For the Anglo-Florentines these villas represented the essence of Florence. Since the eighteenth century, gentlemen on the Grand Tour had popularised images of the city painted from the hill towns of Fiesole, Settignano, Maiano and San Domenico in the north, and San Miniato, Arcetri and Bellosguardo in the south. These panoramas reinforced the idea that Florence was merely the focal point of a vast landscape.

Indeed it was the landscape itself, as much as the villas, which enchanted the Anglo-Florentines. Ruskin wrote to his father in May 1845: 'You cannot conceive what a divine country this is just now; the vines with their young leaves hang as if they were of thin beaten gold – everywhere – the bright green of the young corn sets off the grey purple of the olive hills, and the spring skies have been every one backgrounds of Fra Angelico.' A century later the ageing Bernard Berenson extolled 'the olive-crowned, pine-plumed, cypress-guarded hills…the effect of clouds under the high and spacious dome of the sky'.

In *The Portrait of a Lady*, Henry James, the interpreter *par excellence* of the Anglo-Florentine community, describes his young American protagonist's seduction. 'The air was almost solemnly still, and the large expanse of the landscape, with its gardenlike culture and nobleness of outline, its teeming valley and delicately-fretted hills, its peculiarly human looking touches of habitation, lay there in splendid harmony and classical grace.' Lured by such vistas it is hardly surprising that the Anglo-Florentines retreated to their lofty hilltop villas. There they could imagine themselves as enlightened humanists in the Florence of the Renaissance, not exiles retreating from the expanding industrial city which was, at that very moment, demolishing its picturesque old quarters in a mad dash to modernity.

RIGHT *Florence from the Villa Capponi in the Arcetri district to the south. The dome of the eponymous Duomo – Florence's Cathedral of Santa Maria del Fiore – rises from the valley, creating a focal point for views of the city from the surrounding hills.*

STYLES, SOURCES AND INSPIRATION

*'The delights of an Italian garden are countless. It is not like any other garden
in the world. It is at once more formal and more wild, at once greener with more abundant
youth and venerable with more antique age. It holds Boccaccio between its walls,
all Petrarca in its leaves, all Raffaelle in its skies.'*

OUIDA, Pascarel

THE EARLY ANGLO-FLORENTINES WERE AN AMORPHOUS LOT; with little shared purpose they scattered across the Florentine hills restoring their villas and creating exuberant gardens in isolation. Sir John Temple Leader transformed the ruined fortress of Vincigliata into a robust fantasy castle, while his neighbour Lady Crawford restored her Villa Palmieri in a style more evocative of Boccaccio's ladies than King Arthur's knights. Sir Frederick Stibbert amassed a horticultural hotchpotch of architectural salvage set in an exuberant landscape park, Lady Paget cultivated a cottagey tangle of wild flowers round her austere tower, while Georgina Grahame, displaying the cultural chauvinism of her class, wrested an English flower garden from the recalcitrant Tuscan soil.

Inspired by Millais, Rossetti and Holman Hunt, these early villa dwellers set out to create the simple, informal atmosphere of the medieval garden. While the Pre-Raphaelites provided them with visual inspiration, it was the writings of John Ruskin (1819–1900) which offered the intellectual justification for their approach. Reflecting the Victorian preoccupation with Christianity and self-improvement, Ruskin championed the pious naivety of the Middle Ages over the pagan sensuality of the Renaissance. Ruskin's approach was reinforced by the American scholar Charles Eliot Norton (1827–1908). As Harvard's first professor of art history, Norton virtually introduced Americans to the idea of Italy and certainly shaped late-nineteenth-century attitudes to Italian art. Despite his friendships with Henry James and Edith Wharton – both aficionados of the Baroque, Norton followed Ruskin, extolling medieval art and abhorring all that followed it.

By the late nineteenth century Ruskin's authority was provoking a backlash. In 1865, on his first visit to Italy, the English essayist Walter Pater began to form the Aesthetic Movement which would supplant Ruskin's moralistic approach. Looking beyond the favoured primitive Tuscan painters, Pater discovered the work of Leonardo and Michelangelo, whose undeniable greatness inspired him to advocate aesthetic rather than ethical virtues as the sole criteria for judging art. Catering to a *fin de siècle* hedonism, Pater promoted enjoyment, rather than edification, as the purpose of art, fostering a new appreciation of the Renaissance and Baroque styles.

By the early twentieth century Michelangelo had replaced Giotto as the preferred artist of the Anglo-Florentines and scholarship replaced romance as the guiding force in villa design. This change was brought about largely through the efforts of Janet Ross and Vernon Lee. Long-lived and internationally renowned, these dauntingly erudite women became the Scylla and Charybdis of the expatriate community. Eschewing the fey medievalism of their predecessors they helped wrest art from the clutches of religion. Through numerous scholarly studies, combining literature, history, art and observation, they established a new, intellectual atmosphere. While Ross concentrated on the classical past, Lee focused on the Baroque, producing a series of essays which would enthuse later scholars such as Edith Wharton and Geoffrey Scott.

Encouraged by their example, the Anglo-Florentines began renovating their villas and gardens with an eye to historical accuracy. Most villas retained their essential features and could be easily, if expensively, restored with some semblance of authenticity; the gardens however were generally so decrepit they provided few clues to any original design. Those not actually abandoned had been neglected by locals and tourists alike. In 1872, while exploring the Villa Caprarola, Lady Paget was told by the custodian that she was the first visitor in twelve years; when she stopped at the Villa Manzi the guardian could not recall the last person to visit – not so surprising when one discovers that the owner was a misanthropic old bachelor and the road stopped three miles from the villa. In her 1873 novel *Pascarel*, Ouida's typical Italian garden suggests a languid catalogue of decay: 'old broken marble statues, whence the water dripped and fed the water lily; the great lemon-trees in pots big

enough to drown a boy...marble basins hidden in creepers where the frogs dozed all day long...'.

For those prepared to search, however, there was inspiration to be found. Some gardens, like that of the Villa Capponi, retained the outlines of their Renaissance layout; others, like that at Villa Campi, displayed ancient sculpture and old avenues; an eighteenth-century painting at La Pietra provided an image of the baroque garden, and a garden pavilion at Villa Palmieri preserved a medieval fresco of statuary and topiary. The Medici villas of Pratolino, Poggio a Caiano, Cafaggiolo, Castello, Petraia and Poggio Imperiale survived in various states of decay but the particular favourite of the Anglo-Florentine community was Careggi.

Although the original name, *Campum Regis* (camp of kings), points to Roman occupation, the Anglo-Florentines were seduced by Careggi's humanist associations, as it was the favourite dwelling of Cosimo the Elder. Despite his usurping of the government, they admired Cosimo's liberal views, his patronage of the arts and his interest in classical philosophy. While

ABOVE *George Elgood,* Terrace at Il Palmieri, *c.1907. The exuberant baroque sculpture appears to mimic the architectural evergreens in a harmonious composition that epitomises the Tuscan garden style.*

Harold Acton suggests the wily ruler popularised Neo-Platonism to distract the intellectuals from politics, this seems a little harsh. Like Pliny before him, Cosimo clearly loved country life, and Careggi, located just two miles northwest of the city, provided a convenient rural base. Here he would rise early to plant his vines and prune his fruit trees before attending to affairs of state. In an oft-quoted letter Cosimo writes to Marsilio Ficino: 'Yesterday I arrived at Careggi, not so much with the object of improving my garden as myself,' then chivvies the philosopher to bring with him 'our Plato's book, *De Summo Bono*. This I suppose you have already translated from the Greek into Latin as you promised.'

Cosimo's often illegible letters document the daily routine at the villa where he lived simply, in part to avoid provoking the envy of the citizens over whom he ruled. Janet Ross, who wrote

CASTELLO

ABOVE *Giusto Utens,* Castello, *c.1590 (Museo Storico Topografico Firenze com'era, Florence). Castello's geometric layout and intricate allegorical programme are clearly depicted in Utens' lunette. The flattened birds-eye perspective – something between painting and cartography – enables the artist to create a meticulously detailed depiction of this seminal Medici villa.*

a biography of the Medici family based on such letters, reports that in his final days when Cosimo's wife complained of his silence, he replied: 'When we go to the villa the preparations for our departure occupy thee for fifteen days, dost thou not understand that I who am leaving this life for the next one, have much to think on.'

Although always discreet in his personal manner, Cosimo transformed his fourteenth-century castle into an elegant dwelling; reflecting his humanist ideals, he turned the ancient battlements into a covered arcade to provide splendid views of the surrounding countryside and created a graceful ground floor loggia to link interior with exterior in a manner which would be copied by the Anglo-Florentines half a millennium later. Vasari, that obsequious chronicler of his patron's properties,

reports that the garden was planted to imitate the ancients, with box, bay, cypress, myrtle, pomegranates, quinces, lavender and scented herbs. He also records courtyards, fountains, aviaries, an orchard and an ilex wood, an enclosing wall, a protective moat and a drawbridge – the final three demonstrating the ever-present possibility of insurrection.

Careggi remained a family favourite until 1494 when much of the Medici art collection was looted by the Arrabbiati (the enraged), when they sacked the villa and expelled the family in the first of several revolts. In 1532 the Medici were conclusively returned to power, with the help of the Emperor Charles V, who installed Alessandro de' Medici under the perplexing title of Duke of the Florentine Republic. In the brief spell before his assassination in 1537 Alessandro restored Careggi adding statues, fountains, a maze and a botanical garden. Nonetheless the austere fortress could never suit the luxurious taste of the time.

A century later the estate entered the Anglo-Florentine community, first under the tenancy of Lord Holland, England's ambassador to the Tuscan Court, then later under the Italophile geologist Francis Joseph Sloane. As a consultant for and shareholder in the grand ducal copper mines, Sloane grew wealthy enough to purchase the villa. Although he filled his villa with period furnishings and frescoed the walls with scenes of the humanists, Sloane lacked the horticultural zeal of his compatriots, simply filling his garden with exotic trees and constructing a large *limonaia* to shelter his rare citruses and palms.

Today Careggi houses government offices. Cosimo's ilex woods are surrounded by urban sprawl and a dusty basin and several straight avenues are all that remain of the formal gardens. In its current state it presents a sobering picture of the likely fate of many other Tuscan villas had the Anglo-Florentines not restored them to such splendour that they could later be deployed as academic institutes and tourist enterprises.

At Castello nearby, a second important garden reminded Anglo-Florentine visitors of the horticultural splendours of the past. In 1537, a century after Cosimo the Elder first wrested control of the city from the republic, his descendant, Cosimo I, at the tender age of seventeen, was elected head of the reinstated Florentine Republic before securing himself the title Grand Duke of Tuscany. Later, having cemented his status by marrying his son into Europe's aristocracy, Cosimo set about

transforming the farm on which he had been raised into a villa appropriate to a nobleman. A master of propaganda, he employed the historian Benedetto Varchi to create an iconographical programme which exalted the Medici family and promoted its legitimacy as rulers of Tuscany.

The architect, Niccolò Tribolo, with the work of sculptors Giambologna and Ammanati, translated this programme into a magnificent villa and garden. The farmhouse was extended, the rough orchard slope was landscaped into terraces and hydraulic technology was pioneered to harness distant streams. Physically as well as metaphorically the garden moves from nature to culture, descending through enclosures of increasing sophistication, with a central water course conveying the allegorical programme. Labyrinths, lemon gardens, orchards, flower beds, collections of rare plants, treehouses and other wonders embellish the space, while asserting the wealth, benevolence and power of the ruling family.

With its large, semicircular front forecourt, Castello fulfilled Alberti's prescription for 'ample space for carriages and equestrian exercise', grottoes, cheerful lawns, alleys ending in evergreens, sheltering hedges, stone vases, statues and water

LEFT *Roger Fry,* Giardino di Delizie, *c.1901 (Villa I Tatti, Berenson Collection, Florence). Fry painted his delicate tondo as a marriage present for Mary and Bernard Berenson. With its clever imitation of early Renaissance Gardens of Delight, it is a wry comment on the recherché lifestyle the Berensons created at Villa I Tatti.*

flowing 'from divers places where it is least expected'. With its subtle iconography, its huge collection of modern statuary, its elegant watercourse and its profligate display of rare plants, the garden became legendary in its own time. Vasari described it as the most magnificent in Europe, it spurred Cardinal Ippolito d'Este to create a lavish water garden at his Villa d'Este and even the grudging French essayist Montaigne, who visited in 1580 and again the following year, praised it in his diaries.

Architecturally, however, Castello had barely evolved from the medieval *hortus conclusus*; an enclosed space, it took no advantage of the spectacular views and its simple terracing showed none of the sophisticated architectural staircases, ramps and balustrades of later Renaissance gardens. Nonetheless, because of its rural setting and proximity to Florence, the villa remained within the Medici portfolio and was passed on to the Habsburgs, under whom, as Acton ruefully noted, the villa lost much of its glamour.

In the early twentieth century Edith Wharton condemned Castello as charmless and impersonal, expressing similar contempt for the Boboli Garden, the grandest of the surviving Medici gardens. Since such gardens were designed to assert the power of the governing family they had little relevance to the owners of small private villas; nonetheless, while Wharton waspishly asserts that few spaces display so little of 'that peculiar magic one associates with the old Italian garden', she does concede that the Boboli is 'the most important, if not the most pleasing, of Tuscan pleasure-gardens'.

The Boboli presented a palimpsest of local horticultural trends stretching back over half a millennium. Encompassing more than a hundred acres, the garden provided rural scale in an urban setting, with hills, valleys, woods and meadows all within the city walls. The attendant Pitti Palace had been designed by Brunelleschi in the early fifteenth century on land once owned by a family called Borgoli – a corruption of which gives the garden its name. In 1549 Eleanor of Toledo, wife of the Grand Duke Cosimo I, purchased the property and commissioned her husband's architect to create a formal garden.

Tribolo laid out the dominant axis extending from the vast open piazza in front, through the palace itself and rising up the hill behind to encompass an old stone quarry which he transformed into an amphitheatre for court entertainments. This axis ended in a large reservoir within which a sculpture of the sea god Neptune striking rocks to bring forth water recalled Cosimo's achievement in transporting fresh water from the Apennine hills to fountains throughout the city so that Florentines could enjoy the beneficence of their unelected ruler.

Within a year, Tribolo died, exhausted, it is said, by the sheer scale of the project. The task of completion was taken by

Giorgio Vasari, then Bernado Buontalenti, then Bartolommeo Ammanati. In 1583, after Cosimo's death, his son Francesco I commissioned Buontalenti to create the Grotta Grande. One of the first and the finest of Italy's garden grottoes, this mysterious cavern celebrates the interaction of art, science and nature. Consisting of three chambers encrusted with glittering rocks, intricate shell work and brilliant *trompe l'oeil* painting, the grotto combines the natural with the man-made to create an enchanting, allusive space which appeals to the intellect as much as to the senses.

In the early seventeenth century Cosimo II expanded the garden, transforming the turf amphitheatre into a grand architectural space and creating a second axis in the cypress avenue which runs south towards the Porta Romana. In the eighteenth century when the Medici lands passed to the Habsburgs, the enlightened Pietro Leopoldo opened the gardens to the public, endearing himself forever to the British community. Later grand dukes embellished the garden, constructing the Palazzina della Meridiana to provide more comfortable accommodation and sprinkling the grounds with an Egyptian obelisk, an Austrian *Kaffeehaus* and various greenhouses to support the exotic new plants of the time.

In the nineteenth century the Grand Duke Leopold II – widely despised as an embodiment of foreign rule – constructed the ornate Annalena entrance and a grand new carriage drive. During this period Elizabeth Barrett Browning was a daily visitor, lamenting, all the while, Italian cruelty in barring her beloved cocker spaniel from the grounds. In 1847, the tubercular poet, having eloped from England with her younger lover, settled in the *piano nobile* of the Palazzo Guidi opposite. Their six furnished rooms cost a guinea a week and included admission to the Boboli Garden. Although she spoke little Italian and had few Italian friends, Barrett Browning, like many of her compatriots, ardently promoted Italian independence. When she died in 1861 the city placed a plaque on the Casa Guidi describing her verse as an *aureo anello* – a golden ring wedding Italy and England – thus transforming the Casa Guidi into a pilgrimage stop for British visitors en route to the gardens.

While the Medici villas provided some inspiration to Anglo-Florentines bent on restoration, generally they served architects better than garden makers. For those who wished to reinstate their decaying gardens there were few books on the subject. Visual clues could be gleaned from the illustrations in religious texts, while the backgrounds in paintings by Giotto, Fra Angelico, Ghirlandaio, Gozzoli, Pinturicchio, Botticini and Mantegna chart the evolution of Italian horticulture from the Middle Ages to the High Renaissance. In the mid-eighteenth century Guiseppe Zocchi created a series of etchings of Florence which provided details of many gardens. In 1776 the Swedish

ABOVE *Jacopo del Sellaio*, Banquet of Ahasuerus, *c.1490 (Uffizi Gallery, Florence). The biblical story of Esther convincing the Persian King Xerxes (Ahasuerus) to grant her people freedom was a favourite subject for Renaissance artists. Such paintings provide a rich source of information on contemporary garden features.*

topographical artist F.M.Piper produced a survey of Italian gardens; in 1809 Percier and Fontaine published *Choix des plus célèbres maisons de plaisance de Rome et ses environs* and in 1884 W.P.Tuckerman presented *Die Gartenkunst der Italienischen Renaissance-Zeit*, but none of these were translated into English at the time.

Although many of the Anglo-Florentine garden makers were British, the first modern books on the subject were, in fact, written by Americans. In 1894 Charles Platt published *Italian Gardens*, a slim volume of less than a hundred pages, featuring the novel technique of photography. In its infancy photography was complicated and cumbersome, especially before the invention of flash photography and portable cameras. As late as 1922 Harold Eberlein lamented the impossibility

of securing accurate images 'owing to the fact that the photographer must needs have some appropriate point of vantage on which to plant his camera'.

Platt had no trouble finding vantage points and his photographs provide a romantic impression of decayed elegance. The accompanying text is minimal, superficial, often erroneous and utterly ignores the philosophy and iconography of the gardens.

If Platt's was the first English book on the subject, the most influential was Edith Wharton's 1904 *Italian Villas and their Gardens*. With its exploration of authentic Renaissance style, this book helped shift the Anglo-Florentine approach. Deploring the recent 'Anglicisations', Wharton condemned the 'senseless change' which obliterated ancient terraces, replaced formal alleys with winding paths, turned laurel groves into bamboo thickets, imposed star-shaped beds of begonias and cinerarias and subsumed box parterres beneath rolling lawns that scorched in the searing summer sun. She also condemned the practice of scrubbing statues to unnatural whiteness, destroying the subtle patina with which nature softened the works of man.

With remarkable insight she analysed the balance between mass and void, open spaces and shady enclosures, architectural lines and billowing foliage. Dismissing flowers as 'a parenthetical grace', she asserted that the key elements in Italian horticulture were marble, water and greenery – 'and the achievement, by their skilful blending, of a charm independent of the seasons'. Recognising that Italian gardens had little to do with planting and much to do with design, she fought to include garden plans in the book. Her publisher refused; indeed fearing her text was already too dry, he begged her to add human interest – which she, equally, refused to do. Such omissions notwithstanding, Wharton's book was popular on both sides of the Atlantic. As the book was originally commissioned for serialisation in *Century Magazine*, the editor assumed that Wharton would file poetic prose to complement the nostalgic watercolours of Maxfield Parrish, the fashionable artist he hired to illustrate the work. Although Parrish's dream-like paintings are singularly inappropriate to Wharton's scholarly text, the book sparked a deluge of imitations, most of which copied Platt rather than Wharton, being collections of pretty pictures accompanied by short, impressionistic essays.

The most notable of these is undoubtedly George Sitwell's 1909 *On the Making of Gardens*. Sitwell's essay epitomises the early Anglo-Florentine approach in which romance and nostalgia override any serious scholarship. Unable to see beyond the picturesque decay of the present, Sitwell offers an encomium to the overgrown gardens as they stood in the 1890s rather than making any attempt to discover their original Renaissance spirit. Although he pays little heed to design principles, Sitwell does evoke the pioneering American psychologist William James in a confused attempt to explain the effect of gardens on the human psyche. As his son, Osbert, wryly reports, 'to write a sentence on the psychology of garden making, he would read a hundred slightly obsolete technical volumes.' Although virtually ignored in its time, *On the Making of Gardens* survived to become a perennial favourite and today no self-respecting garden lover would be without it.

BELOW *Fra Angelico,* Annunciation, *c.1430–50 (Museo di San Marco, Florence). A cypress avenue frames the vista beyond the loggias in the Virgin's garden. Born and raised in Tuscany, Fra Angelico is known in Italy as Il Beato Angelico – 'the blessed angelic one', a reference to his painting skills rather than his piety.*

LEFT *Giuseppe Zocchi,*
Gamberaia, *c.1744 (Museo
Storico Topografico Firenze
com'era, Florence). Zocchi's
eighteenth-century etchings of
Tuscany combine charming
narrative vignettes with details
of the architecture, horticulture
and agriculture of theregion.*

Perhaps the most useful and least acknowledged book on the subject is Mrs Aubrey Le Blond's *The Old Gardens of Italy: How to Visit Them* (1912). Although presented as a mere guide, it provides historical background, explores architects and sculptors, describes the gardens and offers tips on how to reach them and to whom to apply for permission to visit. With the modesty of an amateur who feels her social status might be compromised by this foray into commercial publishing, Le Blond is quick to acknowledge the greater expertise of Platt, Wharton and Sitwell, among others.

This plethora of books fuelled a growing interest in Italian gardens, and with such possibilities waiting to be discovered, touring soon became a favourite pastime in the community. Lady Cutting's daughter Iris Origo records that the sight of a cypress avenue leading to a villa would have her mother descending, uninvited, from her chauffeur-driven Lancia and loftily demanding a tour. Sir George Sitwell had a similar attitude, trespassing through private gardens and blithely erecting his umbrella and folding chair while his manservant served champagne and chicken from the ever-present wicker basket. Once, when irate custodians approached, Sitwell attacked them with his umbrella; the long-suffering servant had only to explain that his master was 'an English Signore' and the bruised Italians backed off apologising.

Despite such arrogance, the courage of these early villa visitors should not be underestimated. Brigands lurked in the Italian countryside long after unification and when Lady Paget walked back to her villa at night she took the precaution of arming herself with a revolver and a couple of dogs; 'for the surroundings of Florence are no longer safe to walk about after dark', she explains, before listing the recent murders, attacks and burglaries in the neighbourhood. In an unpublished manuscript Edith Wharton recounts how, while researching the Villa Lante, she was assaulted by a family of cackling lunatics; at another villa she encountered an old lady dying on the sofa. As late as 1912 Le Blond felt compelled to reassure her readers that despite its evil reputation, the forest road to Villa Farnese was now absolutely safe.

Even when travel was no longer treacherous, it remained an arduous business. The roads around Florence were so pitted with potholes that Paget's young son would return from his daily rides caked in mud. Mark Twain describes being hoodwinked by locals who rented him such feeble horses that 'a wheelbarrow' would have been more effective. Georgina Grahame suggested a list of essentials for anyone making an excursion from Florence which included everything from biscuits and brandy to mosquito net, spirit lamp and dark blue calico blinds.

As automobiles were rare at the time, most sites of interest could only be reached by uncomfortable horse carts or slow trains; Wharton reports that she was either rushing through villas in order not to miss her connection or hanging around for hours in musty railway stations. In 1903, after a thrilling 'motor-flight' with America's ambassador to Rome, she resolved to buy her own motorcar, and did so, soon after, on the proceeds of *Italian Villas and their Gardens*.

Motor transport itself remained unreliable for decades. Osbert Sitwell recounts the anxiety over a delayed bus bringing visitors from Siena's 1929 music festival to dine at his father's villa. 'The drivers of the charabancs continually lost their bearings, and wandered hither and thither for hours over Tuscany in the gloaming…. Perhaps they had fallen over a precipice… or one of the drivers might have had a stroke at the wheel, or perhaps he had run amok…?' Indeed it was this very unreliability which introduced the architect Cecil Pinsent to Italy when friends invited him on a motoring holiday to help maintain their vehicle.

While many in the community were diligently recreating Renaissance and Baroque gardens, Cecil Ross Pinsent (1884–1963) began to emerge as a new, modernising force in Anglo-Florentine villa design. A modest, self-effacing man, Pinsent first visited Florence as an architecture student in 1906, during which time he was introduced to the art critic Bernard Berenson. Three years later Berenson's wife Mary, having quarrelled with her Italian architect, persuaded Pinsent to join forces with her current protégé, Geoffrey Scott

ABOVE *Cecil Pinsent and Geoffrey Scott photographed in New York City a few days before Geoffrey Scott's sudden death from pneumonia in August 1929.*

(1884–1929), to take over the restoration of their villa. This commission was to establish Pinsent's career and determine the course of his life. Since many Anglo-Florentines were unable or unwilling to deal with local builders, Pinsent provided an ideal intermediary. As one friend passed him on to another he soon became the favourite architect of the expatriate community.

While Harold Acton noted 'their names were always linked like Chatto and Windus', Geoffrey Scott appears to have contributed little to the partnership. After graduating from Oxford he worked as a librarian for Berenson, during which time he enchanted Mary. Desperate to keep him near, she convinced Pinsent to take him on despite his lack of qualifications. Although Pinsent and Scott lived and worked from a flat in the centre of Florence, Scott spent much of his time at the Berensons' villa, especially after Mary urged him to write a book on architecture. Reflecting the prevailing interest in psychology and aesthetics, he focused on the psychological effect of space and ornament rather than on materials and construction techniques. He also promoted a taste for the Baroque, inspired by the work Vernon Lee had done several decades before. Published in 1914, his *The Architecture of Humanism* was an immediate and enduring success.

During the First World War all pretence of a partnership ended when Pinsent joined the British Red Cross while Scott became press secretary to the British Embassy, then married the wealthy but extremely neurotic Lady Sybil Cutting. At the end of the war Pinsent returned to Florence and resumed his career unimpeded by Scott's indolence. Through the 1920s his commissions ranged from new buildings, through alterations, to garden designs and interior decoration. Meanwhile, politics was overtaking such ephemeral preoccupations. Since coming to power in 1922 Mussolini had attempted to improve his country's agricultural output – not least to offset the sanctions which the west had imposed on his Fascist regime. Along with massive reforestation and land reclamation projects he supported farmers with subsidies, low interest loans and advice on modern agricultural techniques.

In 1931 the government mounted an Italian garden exhibition at the Palazzo Vecchio in Florence. A masterpiece of political propaganda, it celebrated Italian gardens and asserted Italy's horticultural superiority while utterly ignoring the role of the Anglo-Florentines in rediscovering Italian horticulture and rescuing many villas from oblivion. If this was meant as a gauntlet it went unnoticed – indicating, perhaps, the isolation and insularity of the expatriate community.

In the early 1930s, as America's stock market crash was felt in Europe, the Anglo-Florentines scaled down their horticultural projects. The only major building works undertaken by

the community were Sitwell's Montegufoni – which was twenty miles from the city, and Origo's La Foce – even further removed from the urban unrest.

With his base in the city centre and his professional links with the artisan class Pinsent was more conscious than his friends in 'villadom' of the build-up of Fascism. From the mid 1930s he became increasingly disenchanted with his adopted country and just before the outbreak of the Second World War he retired to England. Although his posthumous fame would have amused him, in his three decades in Florence

ABOVE *Pinsent's swimming pool for the Villa Capponi. As the favourite architect of the Anglo-Florentine community Pinsent specialised in inserting modern conveniences into ancient gardens; here end fountains, stone paving, baroque sculpture and high enclosing hedges transform the pool into a baroque water garden.*

Pinsent developed the Anglo-Florentine aesthetic, combining English horticulture, American exuberance and Italian classical design to evolve a modern Tuscan style that was simple, geometric and varied.

THE VILLAS

1
A medieval obsession
SIR JOHN TEMPLE LEADER'S
Villa Maiano and Vincigliata

ABOVE *Among the many illustrious visitors drawn to the castle was Queen Victoria who sketched Temple Leader's Giardino delle Colonne while staying at the Villa Palmieri nearby.*

OPPOSITE *Vincigliata was originally built as one of a line of hilltop fortresses created to defend the city of Florence in the turbulent Middle Ages. Its distinctive profile features in Gozzoli's* Procession of the Magi *in the Palazzo Medici-Riccardi.*

PREVIOUS PAGE *The Villa Medici photographed by Charles Latham, c.1905.*

SIR JOHN TEMPLE LEADER (1810–1903) is the first of what Harold Acton dubbed 'those unmistakable representatives of Albion, who took root among the vineyards and became a part of the landscape'. Having made his fortune in the East India Company and embarked on a promising career as a Whig politician, Temple Leader suddenly quit England and after several years of travel, he settled in Florence. Here he restored not one but two historic properties, the Villa Maiano, a traditional suburban villa, and Vincigliata, a picturesque Gothic castle on the hilltop behind. For both dwellings Temple Leader created simple, imaginative garden settings, but his real horticultural feat was the afforestation of the hillside between them.

Boccaccio's *Decameron* indicates that in the fourteenth century the hills north of Florence were covered in woodlands, meadows and shady springs, the memory of which is preserved in the names of such local villas as La Fonte, La Fontanella and Il Vivaio. In the fifteenth century, this sylvan setting was destroyed by the quarries which sprang up, unchecked, to supply the stone for the city's renaissance. Erosion ensued and by the nineteenth century the region was a lunar landscape of barren scrub. In 1854 John Ruskin described the countryside with his characteristic eloquence as,

> suddenly lonely. Here and there indeed are seen the scattered houses of a farm gracefully set upon the hillside, here and there the fragment of a tower upon a distant rock; but neither gardens, nor flowers, nor glittering palace walls, only a grey extent of mountain ground tufted irregularly with ilex and olive: a scene not sublime for its forms are subdued and low…not rich nor lovely, but sunburnt and sorrowful.

With a quixotic determination to restore his adopted countryside to its medieval splendour, Temple Leader bought up nearly seven hundred acres of land on the hillside, including many farms, a monastery, various villas and several dozen quarries. Although he closed the quarries to halt the erosion and returned the farms to productive cultivation, Temple Leader concentrated, primarily, on reforesting the hills. Planting cypresses in the rocky crevices, filling the arable areas with indigenous pines, oaks, shrubs and wildflowers, and flooding the quarries to create picturesque pools, he shaped the hillside into a naturalistic landscape park.

At the heart of this landscape he created the Giardino delle Colonne, 'garden of the columns', whose name celebrates the fact that the quarry at its centre is reputed to have provided the columns for the church of San Lorenzo. Diverting the Mensola stream, of *Decameron* fame, Temple Leader filled the quarry to create a small lake

which he embellished with a tower, a boathouse, a pier and a tiny altar carved into the rock. He also spanned the bottom of the lake with a massive, medieval-style bridge and erected a two-storey coffee house beyond – inspired, no doubt, by the Boboli's Habsburg *Kaffeehaus* – which he then emblazoned with his own coat of arms.

Whatever whim or indiscretion provoked his sudden departure from England, it did not deter his sovereign from visiting in 1893 while staying at the Villa Palmieri nearby. On 12 April the *Illustrated London News* carried a front-cover engraving of Queen Victoria, attended by her faithful Indian servant, sketching the Giardino delle Colonne. Temple Leader commemorated the event with two large plaques on the coffee house wall – one noting the queen's attendance, the other, his own. Today vandals have destroyed the water garden, the tower is defaced and the boathouse has disintegrated, but Temple Leader's exuberant touch is still evident in a serpentine lily bed at one end of the lake.

Sir John Temple Leader's first Italian residence, the Villa Maiano, sits in front of the forest he so laboriously created. Built in the early fifteenth century for Bartolomeo degli Alessandri, the villa was remodelled repeatedly in its long history, though today it is largely as Temple Leader left it. While respecting Italian traditions, Temple Leader was unable to resist certain English embellishments. The combination he created so epitomises Anglo-Florentine taste that Franco Zeffirelli used the villa as a set for *Tea with Mussolini* – his autobiographical film charting the fortunes of a group of Anglo-American women hanging on in Florence during the Second World War. James Ivory also used it in his film version of E.M.Forster's *A Room with a View*, which depicts an earlier generation of indomitable expatriates.

In 1467, after the original villa was destroyed by a hurricane, the owner sold the estate to pay off his wife's debts. By 1510 the restored villa was in the possession of the influential Pazzi family; under their ownership it was the birthplace of the city's most famous saint, Maria Maddalena, whose writings extol the surrounding country as a haven of peace and tranquility. At the beginning of the eighteenth century when the Pazzi family expired, the villa was acquired by an affluent Sienese textile merchant who added a second storey to reflect his growing status. A century and a half later when Temple Leader bought the property he incorporated the distinctive central turret whose medieval crenellations recall the defensive tower of the Signoria in Florence.

Dramatically perched on the edge of a hillside, the villa was originally approached by the central avenue still visible in the surrounding olive groves. The ramp which today penetrates the enclosing wall and rises, rather aimlessly, through an arched gateway, is the final remnant of this earlier approach. To provide himself with a formal garden, Temple Leader moved the entrance to the side and terraced the land in front of his villa to create two levels. The upper terrace follows the Renaissance tradition, being an open space to balance the solid mass of the architecture. Instead of the traditional Italian gravel however, Temple Leader filled this space with English grass. An ancient wellhead – carefully restored to reveal the crests of earlier owners – predates the formal arrangement and sits off-centre beside one of the paths which bisect the lawn. Flanking almond trees provide shade; a Chinoiserie pavilion to the west invites sunset viewing, while a swimming pool to the east offers views of the surrounding fields. An early exponent of the sport of bathing, Temple Leader would swim in the coldest river or stream and the swimming pool was a precociously modern amenity at odds with his Spartan temperament. Beyond the lawn, Temple Leader built a stone promenade with a balustraded wall, known in its time as the 'viewing terrace', from which to enjoy the spectacular panorama.

BELOW *Temple Leader's first architectural project was to renovate the Villa Maiano, a typical sixteenth-century rural villa to which he added the dramatic medieval-style tower.*

The lower garden, accessed by the original entrance ramp, is more traditionally Italianate. Here gravel paths surround box-edged beds embellished with potted citruses while a nineteenth-century glasshouse leans against the buttressing wall. Today this is an austere space of iris walks, rose-covered walls and grass parterres, though photographs from Temple Leader's time indicate that he had it cluttered with potted exotics and colourful flowers.

When Temple Leader died in 1903, the estate passed to his nephew, Lord Westbury, who broke up the property and sold it in pieces. Subsequent owners have respected Temple Leader's restoration and today the villa is owned by an Italian countess who preserves the Anglo-Florentine flavour, capitalising on its charm by renting out the villa for courses, weddings and other events.

Like many born during the Industrial Revolution, Temple Leader followed the Pre-Raphaelites in their passion for the Middle Ages. Exploring an earlier Anglo-Florentine connection, he wrote a book about the fourteenth-century mercenary John Hawkwood, who, like Temple Leader himself, married a local woman in later life and settled in the region. In 1855, ten years after purchasing the Villa Maiano, he undertook his second architectural restoration, the medieval Castello di Vincigliata. This picturesque ruin, towering over the Maiano hills, had been sacked in the fourteenth century by none other than Hawkwood himself in the pay of the Pisans.

As with the best Anglo-Florentine villas, the castle has an illustrious heritage, its original owners having been the Usimbardi, who, among other claims to fame, were friends of Dante. After its destruction by Hawkwood the castle was rebuilt in 1368 by Nicolo degli Alessandri, whose granddaughter later married Giovanni de' Medici. Over time, the Alessandris' power waned and the estate fell into disrepair. By 1637 the owner, who cared only for hunting, was squatting in a corner of the castle with his young son and an ancient aunt. Several years later the youth and his page were the sole inhabitants, and by 1751 the local church registry recorded that nobody lived in the ruined dwelling but every Easter holy water was sprinkled in the empty rooms.

While it is often billed as a restoration, Temple Leader's efforts at Vincigliata amount to a complete re-creation. Henry James wryly noted, 'Vincigliata is a product of the millions, the leisure and the eccentricity…of an English Gentleman.' Although planned with the help of a local architect, Giuseppe Francelli, it appears that

LEFT *Behind its heavy wooden gates, Vincigliata is filled with architectural salvage, much of it scavenged from the late-nineteenth-century urban regeneration projects which replaced the medieval heart of Florence with modern buildings.*

the patron really was the imaginative force behind the design, not least because the architect died long before the project was finished.

Though James declares it 'a triumph of aesthetic culture', Vincigliata has no precedent in Tuscan architecture. Its turrets, grotesques, coats of arms, iron braziers and instruments of torture have a distinctly theatrical air. Nonetheless, in recreating the castle, Temple Leader preserved ancient crafts by employing local stonemasons, carpenters, sculptors and glassmakers. Further, in 1865 when large parts of the city were being demolished, he rescued many architectural relics to incorporate into his castle. While today such opportunism would be considered cultural theft, if Temple Leader had not purchased the artefacts they would have been lost forever.

In creating a garden for his medieval fantasy Temple Leader was equally inventive. While a real fourteenth-century castle garden would have been a dirty, crowded, smelly enclosure of donkeys, cows, scratching fowl, a few vegetables and perhaps a patch of cereal, Temple Leader created a rather Pre-Raphaelite space, combining roses, colourful flowers and picturesque architectural relics. Above a cobbled ramp the massive doors, guarded by stone lions, open on to a small grass lawn. In true English fashion Temple Leader softened the enclosing walls with climbing roses and added a central fountain surrounded with further rose beds, enclosed in box-edged parterres, topiary cones, gravel paths and potted citruses.

The castle itself is built round an austere courtyard, appropriately devoid of greenery, but embellished with a central well which sports a dragon-held pulley that owes more to gothic fantasy than any local tradition. An upper terrace, accessed by a steep stone staircase, offers magnificent views of the surrounding woods – created by Temple Leader himself – with Florence glittering in the distance.

Abutting the lawn is another eccentricity – a sunken cloister which Temple Leader designed, complete with frescoes of historical scenes from the lives of the castle's earlier owners. Though the only surviving image depicts Uglino de Visdomini invoking the Virgin before setting off to fight the Sienese, one wonders what gallant scene Temple Leader commissioned from his own life, since he carefully insinuated his imprimatur throughout the estate, embellishing the farms with his monograms and crests and incorporating into the castle wall itself a Della Robbia-style terracotta plaque of the Virgin against the crests of himself and his wife.

While Temple Leader remained in the relative comfort of Villa Maiano, he placed his Italian in-laws in the castle above. Even when inhabited, however, the place continued to exude a sinister aura. In 1913, from his villa down the hill in San Domenico, Joseph Lucas noted that not even the July sun drenching its towers could soften 'the expression of forbidding sternness and hostility stamped deeply on the haggard face of that feudal stronghold'. Fittingly, during the Second World War the castle served as a prison for English officers. Today, like so many of the grand Anglo-Florentine villas, it has become a venue for weddings and conferences.

There is some irony in the fact that Temple Leader, having been a radical member of parliament, spent so much of his time and money recreating a feudal atmosphere. Nonetheless, his faux medieval gardens and fantasy castle reflect the early Anglo-Florentine preoccupation with romance over scholarship while his heroic restoration of the barren hillside reveals an extraordinary affection for the Tuscan landscape. Today the Bosco di Vincigliata is a public park, overseen by the commune of Fiesole. As so often occurs in the annals of Anglo-Florentine history, however, the local literature makes no acknowledgement of the eccentric English aristocrat who created their prized woodland just over a century ago.

RIGHT *Vincigliata broods over the hillside feeding the fantasies of generations of romantic Anglo-Florentines; as Henry James declared: 'The massive pastiche of Vincigliata has no superficial use…so disinterested and so expensive a toy is its own justification; it belongs to the heroics of dilettantism.'*

2
A Virgilian fantasy
JANET ROSS' Poggio Gherardo

ABOVE *Ross' private sitting room was filled with portraits, sketches and the desk she inherited from her mother. Here she would retreat each morning from the social life of the villa to work on farm accounts; in the evenings she would return to her correspondence, research and writing.*

OPPOSITE *Ross' niece Lina Waterfield and her friend Madge Addington Symonds on the garden steps at Poggio Gherardo. Madge's father, John Addington Symonds, was one of many who benefited from Ross' famed hospitality, staying at the castle for weeks at a time while researching his seminal* The Life of Michelangelo Buonarroti.

ALTHOUGH SHE HAD NO GARDEN TO SPEAK OF, Janet Ross (1842–1927) was one of the first, and most influential, of the Anglo-Florentine community. For nearly forty years she presided from the medieval fortress of Poggio Gherardo – *poggio* meaning a hill, Gherardo, the name of the venerable Florentine family which acquired the property in 1433 and from whom the Rosses purchased it four and a half centuries later. Surrounded by vineyards, olive groves, vegetable gardens and ilex woods, Poggio exemplified the *villa rustica* described in classical treatises. Virgil was never far from Ross' thoughts and his *Georgics* shaped her working practice. While many photographs of the time depict teas, balls and garden parties, Ross' album, faithfully preserved in the British Institute in Florence, offers a catalogue of harvests, peasants, boisterous dogs and those patient, statuesque, lake-eyed oxen of which the Anglo-Florentine community was so fond.

Born to the adventurous traveller, Lucie Duff Gordon, Janet Ross rejected George Meredith as an early suitor, although she was delighted when the love interest in his 1860 novel *Evan Harrington* proved to be an independent young woman with a marked resemblance to herself. At the age of eighteen the headstrong Janet married Henry Ross, an affluent banker twenty-two years her senior. As Ross was a partner in the Alexandria-based Briggs and Co. bank, Janet moved with him to Egypt and for three years acted as Egypt correspondent for *The Times*. In 1866 the bank went bankrupt – victim of a general downturn in Egypt's economy when the close of the American Civil War ended Egypt's monopoly on selling cotton to Manchester's mills.

With most of their savings lost the Rosses retreated to England where their only child, Alick, was being raised by a great aunt. Unable to survive in style on their diminished finances, they moved on to Florence, renting apartments in the centre where they could continue to live elegantly despite their reduced circumstances. In 1870 when the capital moved to Rome, 30,000 courtiers, diplomats, politicians and businessmen followed, depriving Florence of much of its social and intellectual vigour. Like many disillusioned by the increasing modernisation of the city, the Rosses decided to try country life. In Lastra a Signa, a small town to the southwest, they rented a wing in the Villa Castagnolo, ancient home of the Marchese Lotteringo della Stufa. The Marchese, known to his friends as Lotti, was a decade younger than Henry and he and Janet became fast friends. While many speculated on the intimacy between them, others believe Janet's interest in men was always essentially intellectual.

As court chamberlain to the constitutional monarch, King Victor Emmanuel, Lotti was obliged to spend much of his time in Rome so Janet gradually took over the running of the estate. The trio coexisted happily, and in 1888, when Lotti became terminally ill, Janet nursed him till the end. On his death, however, the Rosses were obliged to quit the villa as the Marchese's family had always found the arrangement uncomfortably unorthodox.

On the hill below Settignano north of Florence, the Rosses discovered Poggio Gherardo. Although it was suffering from decades of neglect, they purchased the property, and Janet, at forty-six, acquired her first real home. The villa interior had been adapted over the centuries, providing, among other rarities, a room with French windows on to a balcony which Ross used as a study, and another whose walls were covered with eighteenth-century *trompe-l'oeil* landscapes. A bathroom was created from the chapel and bemused visitors lying in the bath would find themselves staring up at a dove painted on the ceiling.

Unlike most of her cohort, Ross had little interest in gardening. A simple stone terrace to the east was surrounded by marble banquettes shaded by a grape pergola in imitation of the outdoor dining tables depicted in Roman mosaics. The terrace itself was enclosed by a simple metal fence, rather than the usual stone balustrade – suggesting a lack of interest, finances or both. A wisteria shaded the balcony outside Ross' study, beneath which was a grotto and pool filled with Burmese goldfish probably supplied by Lotti who had, in his youth, spent time in Burma overseeing the building of the Rangoon–Mandalay railway. Descendants of these fish still graced Harold Acton's ponds in the 1970s, although, as he ruefully admitted, careless breeding over the years had lost them their elegant rococo tails. Around the grotto a broad parterre was planted with exotic trees such as medlar, magnolia, persimmon and a large camphor tree which scented the air. Lemon trees in terracotta pots surrounded the gravel terrace along the villa's main entrance; apart from these however, Ross confined her floral embellishment to a few potted exotics and some flowering shrubs such as oleander, hydrangea and plumbago, around which her gardener would carefully construct little mounds to contain the precious water.

Although he barely figures in the chronicles of the time, Henry Ross was described by his niece, Lina Waterfield, as modest, decent, and a spellbinding storyteller. The vividness of his descriptions, the elegance of his prose and his subtle appreciation of the orient were revealed in the volume *Letters from the East – 1837-57* which his wife compiled, edited and had published in 1902, the year of his death.

Although his primary interests were cultivating rare orchids and raising guinea pigs, Henry is credited with planting the barren hillside beneath the castle to resemble the landscape described in Boccaccio's *Decameron*. Unlike their neighbour, Temple Leader, the Rosses made no effort to create a natural-looking wood; their arboreal treasures included such rare specimens as eucalyptus, Japanese loquats, azaleas, moutan peonies and two twelve foot high Japanese kaki trees. A vine-covered pergola lined with lilies provided a shady path from the villa to the road while the main gate was marked with double gate-posts topped with busts of the four seasons.

An article about the estate in the 1912 *Gardeners' Chronicle* portrays a negligent tangle in which 'roses luxuriate everywhere…forming a wealth of floral tracery'. It also notes the wisteria is growing in such profusion that it threatens to pull down the staircase leading from the terrace to the vineyards below.

Between cultivating her land and entertaining a stream of political and literary luminaries, Ross also managed to write more than

BELOW *From this elegant gate with its busts of the four seasons the entrance avenue at Poggio Gherardo winds up to the castle lined with purple leaved* Prunus pissardii, *embellished with an inner hedge of red roses and a ribbon of scented blue irises.*

a dozen books on subjects ranging from Tuscan cooking through Florentine palaces to a study of the Medici – a heroic task gleaned from letters of the time, where the difficult feat of translation was exacerbated by archaic script, idiosyncratic spelling and illegible handwriting. What began as an attempt to generate extra money with short articles for publications such as *Frazer's Magazine* and *The English Illustrated Magazine* soon turned into a vocation as Ross discovered a talent for writing, an interest in research and a loyal audience for her work.

In her literary output Ross competed for supremacy with her formidable neighbour Vernon Lee, about whom she once averred, 'such ugliness should be a mortal sin'. Although Ross might have felt threatened by her rival's overt lesbian lifestyle, Lee was not, by any means, the sole recipient of her acerbic tongue. Among the many other women for whom she had little time was the eccentric novelist known as Ouida. While Ouida vied for the affections of Lotti, the antipathy between the two women reached its climax when Ross had one of Ouida's dogs put down for biting her son. Ouida retaliated by creating a vituperative portrait of Ross in her 1878 *Friendship*. Here in the guise of Lady Joan Challoner, Ross is presented as a snobbish, greedy, manipulative adulteress whose accommodating husband colludes in her schemes to sell fake antiquities to gullible tourists. Since Ouida presented the expatriate community as idle and hypocritical, her book was denounced and she was ostracised. Nonetheless, her portrait cannot be wholly inaccurate as Georgina Grahame in her 1902 *In a Tuscan Garden* also wrote, rather snidely, of Ross:

> She no longer traffics in 'Murillos' and 'Peruginos' with the names of these painters inscribed in large gold letters on their frames – all to be sold for the benefit of distressed Italian families – but has turned her attention to pastoral pursuits, and places her oil and wine on the English market, no doubt as much to the advantage of her customers as to her own, which could hardly be said of the old line of business.

Ouida depicts Lady Challoner's 'pastoral pursuits' as the desecrating of her Italian lover's ancestral estate by cutting walks, erecting fences, importing English livestock, planting English trees, replacing picturesque farm buildings with modern breeding-pens and glazing the elegant loggia to fill it with hot-house exotics. While this grotesque portrait doubtless describes the cumulative heresies of many Anglo-Florentines, it bears very little resemblance to Ross. As Ouida preferred Paris gowns to Wellington boots and literary salons to vegetable plots, she was in no position to comment on Ross' agricultural activities. Furthermore, it is unlikely that Lotti would have allowed Ross to manage his estate for nearly two decades if he had not been happy with the results. In her novel however, Ouida is scathing about her protagonist's hands-on approach:

> She dug and planted, and bought and sold, and planned and bargained; she kept a sharp eye on the weights and measures, she ran up model styes and breeding-pens; she got up at five to count the potatoes and melons, the cherries and cabbages that went to the market; she rode (her lover's) horses, and ordered his bailiffs and strode about in grey linen and big boots, and did on the whole most admirably – for herself.

Through such efforts the real life Ross managed to support a staff of nine, entertain in memorable fashion and maintain a large villa stuffed with books, antiques and art.

Although farming is an essential element in the classical idea of villa life, the Anglo-Florentines generally had little interest in working the land. Those whose estates contained several farms would generally hire a manager or lease their fields to nearby farmers.

As one of the few members of the community to engage in the business of farming, Ross ran her estate on the ancient *mezzadria* or 'half and half' system in which tenant farmers, known as *contadini,* provided the labour and shared the profits, while the landowner supplied the capital, providing the land, maintaining the farm buildings and covering half the cost of livestock, seed, fertiliser and machinery. The *contadini* were a major feature of expatriate villa life although many had a difficult relationship with these locals on whom they were so dependent.

From the time of ancient Rome, Italy's rural villas had been expected to support the owner's family, supplying his rural and urban households, while creating a surplus to sell. In small estates like Poggio Gherardo, the relationship between landowner and staff was close emotionally as well as physically. While Ross sent figs, melons and artichokes to market in the first year, her *contadini* taught her to harvest from the countryside as well, gathering wild garlic, chestnuts, mushrooms and truffles to supplement cultivated crops and ensure enough produce to dry or conserve from one year to the next. In those days mushrooms were gathered into wicker baskets which allowed the spores to disperse, while the truffles that proliferate in Tuscany's chestnut woods were harvested with dogs rather than the traditional pigs – the latter being more likely to gobble the precious fungi before it can be collected.

Poggio Gherardo contained three farms, known as *podere.* The largest of these, sited by the main gate, was leased by a *contadino* with the picturesque name of Adamo Innocenti. In the typical Tuscan manner, the ground floor of his house served as a storeroom with the living quarters on the floor above. There was also a barn where the wine-making equipment was kept, and a stable housing a few milk cows plus a pair of sturdy oxen. All three buildings gave on to a stone courtyard where maize, pumpkins and melons would ripen while tomatoes, peaches and figs were laid out to dry in the autumn sun. Adamo's brother, Cesare, leased the farm halfway up the hill which housed the *frantoio* or olive press, while a third farm was found at the back of the hill.

While the many writers within the community were inspired by rural life, those with first-hand experience exploited it to great effect. Their descriptions of seasonal rituals are virtually unchanged from those recorded in classical texts. Early spring was given over to ploughing, then the sowing of clover and corn. In March the lambs were born; when they were weaned the peasant women would make the chalky pecorino cheese which tasted of wild thyme from the sheep's grazing grounds. After hay-making in May, and the June harvesting and threshing of grain, there was little to do through the heat of summer. In autumn things became busy again with the 'Sunday fusillade' when men would skip Mass to hunt boar, pheasant, rock-doves and other smaller birds – a pastime favoured by the middle classes since few peasants could afford guns. Although Ross herself was partial to shooting, the practice was widely deplored in the expatriate community; Lady Paget even petitioned the archbishop to order parish priests to preach against the slaughter of small birds.

Notwithstanding the distractions of the hunt, farm work continued in earnest with the grape-picking in September, followed by the autumn harvest of wheat and a late

sowing of grain. The year culminated in the gathering of olives, the pressing of oil and the winemaking – an activity which provoked a quasi-religious delight among the expatriate community.

Despite its hallowed status, the Tuscan vineyard required almost constant attention. In spring the rows between the vines had to be hoed; pruning was done when the danger of frosts was over, the pruned shoots being tied with switches of willow while the clippings were saved for kindling. After the wind, storms and drought of summer the approach of the *vendemmia* or grape harvest was marked by the repairing of the casks and vats.

In an article written in 1874 for *Macmillan's Magazine,* Ross described the harvest at Lotti's estate. 'On a fine September morning we started, Italian and English, men and women, masters and mistresses, and servants laden with innumerable baskets…'. She goes on to recount how the 'padrona', a portrait of herself, would serenade the workers with Tuscan folk songs till lunch arrived from the villa: 'a steaming dish of risotto con fungi', a 'knightly' sirloin of beef, a large 'fiasco' or straw-bound bottle of red wine tempered with water from a neighbouring well. Meanwhile the labourers feasted nearby on the rare luxury of white beans and sausage.

Although many expatriates were content simply to watch the activity, well into her eighties Ross would oversee the harvest, drafting in friends and visitors as well as the families of her staff. On the chosen morning the workers would gather with boxes and secateurs, wearing hats to keep the earwigs from falling in their hair and gloves against the wasps hiding in the vines.

The grapes were dumped from individual collecting boxes into large chestnut-wood tubs placed along the vine rows. When full, these were loaded on to heavy ox-drawn carts and transported to the cavernous room in the farmyard where young men would mount the ladders to tip the grapes into huge vats. When the vats were full, the men, having rolled up their trousers and washed their feet, would tramp on the grapes. Despite the danger of intoxication, Ross recorded, 'it is an article of faith that the perfume of the must is the best medicine and people bring weakly children to…breathe the fume-laden air'. After the wine had been transferred to barrels, the frugal Tuscans would re-ferment the remaining pulp with water to make a light wine known as *mezzo vino*.

Although less celebrated than the *vendemmia*, the olive harvest was just as important. Ross' olive groves were arranged in terraces cut into the hillside; any flat land between the vines was turned over to hay, which, in respect of local superstition, would not be harvested before 24 June, the feast day of San Giovanni, patron saint of Florence. Olives were harvested between late November and early January before the winter winds could cause the ripe fruit to drop and bruise. Only tree-picked fruit could be used for virgin oil, although windfalls were used for second pressings. As with the *vendemmia*, on the appointed day every able-bodied person would be drafted in, gathering the olives in wicker baskets strapped round their waists. These were then dumped into barrels which would be transported to the press – a heavy millstone, turned by a donkey or horse, blindfold to prevent it from getting dizzy.

Windfalls were used in the second pressing; a third pressing provided oil for soap, and the final pulp – a dark brown cake – was used as fuel or fertiliser. The oil itself would rest in terracotta urns for several weeks before being distributed between farmer and tenants; it would then be stored in cellars, carefully separated from the wine to prevent the flavours from mixing.

While it was less glamorous than the timeless groves or sacred vineyards, Ross also kept a vegetable garden which was large enough to supply her own and her tenants' families with a surplus to sell in the market in Florence. Unlike many of her com-patriots who bemoaned Italian cooking and imported their own chefs, Ross celebrated the local cuisine and in 1899 she wrote a cookbook, *Leaves from our Tuscan Kitchen* which was republished in 1973, edited and updated by her great great nephew, Michael Waterfield.

Predating by over half a century Elizabeth David's discovery of the Mediterranean, Ross' book is one of the first English cookbooks to present cooking as an art. Her erudite introduction meanders from a medieval recipe for stuffed goose to the proper way to cook peacocks – which is skinned, not plucked, so the cooked bird can be recloaked in its finery for serving. Whether she is describing the various mushrooms found in the Tuscan hills or recording the season for Genoese asparagus, the book reveals her profound love of the local countryside.

While happy to advise on vegetables, Ross carefully guarded the secret of her famous vermouth, the making of which she developed into a profitable industry. Although she claimed to have found 'an old Medici recipe', the base of the vermouth was simply a strong white wine, imported from Sicily, as Ross' own wine did not have the requisite fifteen per cent alcohol. To this Ross would add sugar, a secret blend of thirteen herbs marinated in alcohol and a mixture of three bitters including the wormwood – *ver muth* – which gives the drink its name.

ABOVE *Unlike many of her cohort, Ross did nothing to alleviate the austere façade of her dwelling. Its square battlements were a sign of allegiance to the Guelph faction in the protracted battles between pope – supported by the Guelphs – and emperor – supported by the Gibbelines, which raged throughout the Middle Ages.*

Although Ross made less than a hundred cases a year, her vermouth was renowned far beyond the community. Some cases were shipped to friends in England like Hilaire Belloc, others went to local wine merchants such as the proprietor of 'Old England' – the spiritual home of the nostalgic expatriate. The majority of each year's produce, however, was sold through the wine department of London's Army and Navy Stores.

One of Ross' many claims to fame within the Anglo-Florentine community was her assertion that her defensive castle was the palace to which Boccaccio's youthful protagonists retire in the *Decameron*. Modern scholars believe Boccaccio invented an idealised country retreat, but if he was inspired by an actual dwelling Ross' austere fortress has neither the spacious courtyard nor the elegant loggias of his description. While it did contain a well 'of cool refreshing water' and 'cellars stocked with precious wines', such features are found in almost any rural residence. The nearby villa of Il Palmieri has a greater claim as Boccaccio's model, being closer to Florence, more palatial and sited beside the Mensola stream which is mentioned in the novel; indeed the fact that its Anglo-Florentine owner, Lady Crawford, was widely known as 'Lady Boccaccio' must have irritated the competitive Mrs Ross.

Whatever Poggio's true history, its dramatic crenellations, venerable vineyards and picturesque terrace, were an inspiration to the community. As, indeed, was its chatelaine, whose love of local custom and study of Italian history shaped the Anglo-Florentine approach to their host country. At the end of the nineteenth century Bernard Berenson had stayed with Ross at Poggio Gherardo while his villa I Tatti was being rebuilt – a project made possible by a loan from Ross. Although he was never one to acknowledge mentors, this period must have influenced the impressionable youth, who, like his hostess, was later to supplement his income by dealing, subtly, in old masters. The American writer Mark Twain also enlisted Ross' help to secure the Villa Viviani in Settignano which he rented in 1892 while writing *Pudd'nhead Wilson*. Twain describes looking down from his windows on to 'the imposing mass of the Ross castle, its walls and turrets rich with the mellow weather-stains of centuries…'.

During the First World War, when many Anglo-Florentines fled to the safety of their homelands, the septuagenarian Ross stayed on, sharing her requisitioned villa with Italian officers, overseeing the welfare of her staff, running her farms on the labour of old men as the young men had all been conscripted, and sending news to Mary Berenson who waited anxiously in England.

Ross' letters record heat, drought and boredom. On 26 August 1918 she writes, 'Dear Mary. It is awfully hot, which is not fresh news,' she then goes on to describe her nephew's operation. A day later she begins: 'Hot, hot, hot. That is my news…', then she reports that one of Mary's *contadini* has been taken prisoner and she will send him a sack of bread every month. 'I have four prisoners to whom I send, none of whom I know, but they are relatives of some of my people.' Such concern for the local people was rare among the expatriates and Ross was repaid, for the most part, by the lifelong devotion of her coachman, cellarman, two gardeners, lodge keeper, odd job man, cook and lady's maid. The only exception was her household steward, who, after her death, was revealed to have been stealing her exclusive vermouth and selling it in Florence under his own label.

After the armistice, however, the situation changed. Italy's huge death toll and legions of disabled veterans, coupled with widespread unemployment and food shortages generated anger in the local population, much of which was directed at foreigners and rich landowners. Centuries-old customs were challenged and alliances were severed; Ross' own gardener, after decades of loyal service, even threatened to strike for better wages, though he was soon talked round. Worse still, in July 1919 a mob from the local village of Monte a Mensola mounted the hill and raided Ross' cellar taking wine, oil and maize. The fact that these were local men made the incident even more upsetting

In the early 1920s, after the Bolshevik Revolution in Russia, small Communist parties began forming throughout Europe. One group of red-flag-waving demonstrators confronted the aged Ross who rebuked them with such a stream of abuse that they scattered in terror. Ironically, the real danger, Fascism, went largely unnoticed and Ross was one of many Anglo-Florentines who felt that Mussolini's promise of stability might be worth backing. In 1927, at the age of eighty-five, she died, before the spectacle of Mussolini stirring up his blackshirts could confound her expectations.

Towards the end of her life, on learning that her son had run up huge bills on the prospect of inheriting Poggio, Ross changed her will. To ensure that her property would not be sold to pay off his debts, she left the estate to her great nephew, with a life interest to her niece and ward, his mother, Lina Waterfield.

Having braved her aunt's disapproval to marry the English painter Aubrey Waterfield, Lina had retreated with her husband to the Fortezza della Brunella, a moated, medieval fortress at Aulla in the Lunigiana region of northwestern Tuscany. Ross' steward declared the dwelling unfit for Christians, while the local villagers believed it was haunted by the ghosts of soldiers massacred there in the eighteenth century. Undeterred, the Waterfields restored the castle with its massive, sixteen foot deep walls. More impressive still, Aubrey created a garden on the roof, in the earth which the Spanish garrison had painstakingly carted up there a century before to absorb the kick from its cannons.

Fixing a primitive pulley to one of the square corner towers, Aubrey hauled up wicker baskets of fertiliser and plants to create an ilex avenue, a vine-clad pergola, a rosemary hedge and box-edged, flower-filled parterres. The focal point was a rose-covered, white-trellised pavilion, in front of a lily pond which framed a view of the Carrara mountains beyond. Unfortunately nothing remains of this horticultural fantasy. When the family eventually attempted to sell after Lina's death the fortress was compulsorily purchased by the government and after an unsuccessful attempt at restoration it was left to disintegrate.

When Janet Ross died in 1927, the Waterfields reluctantly quit Aulla and moved to Poggio Gherardo to manage the estate. They were already familiar figures in the Anglo-Florentine community as Lina had been one of the founders of the British Institute. In 1917 when antagonism towards foreigners was rising, she and several other members of the expatriate community had formed a library and cultural centre to promote a better understanding of English culture. Like her guardian, Lina Waterfield was both a journalist and writer, acting as the Italian correspondent for the *Observer* from 1921–39, and producing several guidebooks to Italian cities.

In their effort to pay the taxes on Poggio, the Waterfields turned the villa into a 'finishing school' for English girls. The upstairs rooms were transformed into dormitories

BELOW *The 'sky garden' Aubrey Waterfield created on the roof of the fortezza was the focus of family life through the summer as it received the breeze funnelled up the valley from the sea.*

ABOVE *The Fortezza della Brunella in northwest Tuscany was an ancient military fortress with massive walls, square towers at each corner and a spectacular view of the Carrara mountains beyond.*

holding around a dozen borders; a friend from the local university was drafted in to teach Italian language and literature; Lina herself taught Italian history and Aubrey taught drawing and painting. Bernard Berenson opened his library to the girls, and the Waterfields' daughter, Kinta, recently graduated from school in England, obtained a driving licence to chauffeur their charges to sites of interest.

The school was successful in the early years, but by the mid-1930s, with the rise in Fascism, English parents became increasingly uneasy about sending their daughters to Italy. Despite the warnings of impending war the Waterfields were reluctant to leave, delaying their departure until it was nearly too late.

Like many large estates in the region Poggio was requisitioned, first by Senator Morelli, a prominent Fascist, and later by American troops. After Morelli's retreat with the Germans, almost everything of value had disappeared, including letters from D.H. Lawrence and Lucie Duff Gordon. While considerably more respectful, the Americans who then inhabited the villa covered one of the eighteenth-century frescoes with white paint to create a movie screen, assuming that the owners would want to 'redecorate' when they repossessed the place.

After the war the septuagenarian Lina, now a widow, returned to Poggio, determined to restore the estate. Although the land was littered with unexploded mines, it was civil unrest more than hidden weapons which caused the greatest anxiety. With the departure of British and American troops, reports began to circulate that the Communists were plotting a coup. Ironically, amid cries of '*La terra ai contadini*', the *contadini* themselves turned their backs on the land. Young men quit the isolation and labour of the farm for easier work in factories, shops and tourist industries. Young women, having tasted urban independence, refused to return to the cramped, dirty, crowded farms.

For villa owners, even where domestic staff and farm labour could be procured, food was in short supply as farm produce was requisitioned by regional authorities for distribution in the cities. By 1946 farmers were allowed to keep most of their produce with only a kilo of oil per olive tree being requisitioned against shortages. To finance the villa, Lina opened it to paying guests, where it soon became a favourite among English visitors still suffering food rationing at home.

The post-war scarcity of materials delayed repairs at Poggio, as elsewhere. During the war most of the vines had died through neglect, although only a few dozen of the 700 olive trees had been destroyed, and those were lost in artillery duels across the Arno valley. More dispiriting however, the Fascist officer had dug up and sold the several thousand irises which lined the drive – their roots being a valuable ingredient in the manufacture of perfume and soap.

Eventually, however, with the premature death of her son to whom Ross had left the estate, Lina Waterfield, was forced to sell Poggio. It was purchased by a developer who promised he would not divide up the property, then promptly did so, separating the villa and its three farms. The terraced olive groves were soon obliterated by housing while the villa was sold to a religious order which used it as an orphanage. Although the grounds are now neglected Poggio's crenellated profile still towers, intriguingly, from the road below. Despite Ross' selfconsciously Virgilian lifestyle, the fortress continues to evoke the rough turbulence of the Middle Ages – its seventy-year Anglo-Florentine phase but a brief interlude in the villa's long history.

3
Paradise lost
Villa Palmieri

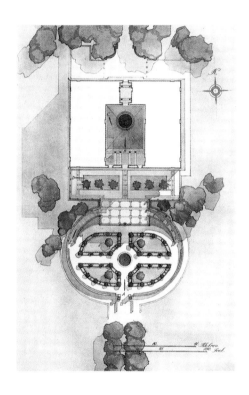

THE VILLA PALMIERI, in the village of San Domenico, was said to be one of the villas to which Boccaccio's youthful protagonists fled the 1348 plague. Though modern scholars believe Boccaccio invented his locations, Il Palmieri certainly conforms to his description. Sited on 'an eminence', it boasts 'a spacious courtyard, loggias and halls', surrounded by 'delectable gardens and meadows'. If Boccaccio was simply expressing the fourteenth-century image of Eden, the Anglo-Florentine community happily promoted the idea that Il Palmieri was that place, especially as several of their number owned the villa at different times.

Throughout the early twentieth century, garden guides, both English and American, quoted vast swathes of the *Decameron* in their entries on the villa; Arthur Bolton's 1919 *The Gardens of Italy* even suggests the estate was earlier owned by Dante's father, based on a 1336 contract in the city archives. Bolton too, however, concentrates on Boccaccio, claiming that it was still possible to identify the scenes in which he set his stories.

Whether based on reality or fiction, Boccaccio's detailed description of the villa's gardens provided inspiration to generations of horticulturists. Its catalogue of long, spacious walks, vine-hung pergolas, scented citrus trees, a central lawn dotted with 'a thousand different kinds of gaily-coloured flowers' and a central marble fountain shooting 'a wondrous water jet' was self-consciously reproduced in many Anglo-Florentine gardens.

Though built in the thirteenth century, the villa was extended in the mid fourteenth century, when a loggia was added, either inspired by or inspiring Boccaccio's 'fair gallery' with its view of the flowery courtyard in which his protagonists take their first breakfast banquet.

In 1454 the estate was purchased by Matteo Palmieri, whose grandfather, a successful apothecary, had made his fortune by investing in real estate. Matteo himself was a leading humanist, friend of Cosimo the Elder and a prolific writer in both Latin and the vernacular Italian. In 1475 he commissioned Botticini to paint *The Assumption of the Virgin* (National Gallery, London) in which the villa features behind him and his wife. Though painted more than a hundred years after Boccaccio's description, the villa here appears a modest dwelling with no garden at all. While Matteo, in the painting, wears the robes of a successful politician he was later condemned as a heretic for his views on free will expressed in his most famous work *La Citta di Vita*, the City of Life. Despite this ignominy, the family name supplanted the villa's earlier names, *Schifanoia*, meaning 'banish care', and *Fonte de Tre Visi*, 'Fountain of three vistas', both of which suggest the estate must have been idyllically sited, whether or not it contained a garden.

LEFT *Giuseppe Zocchi,* Villa Palmieri, *c.1744. Zocchi's etching shows the old Florence/Fiesole road bisecting the estate and passing beneath the balustraded south terrace created a century before to exploit the views of the city.*

In the 1630s, during one of the many plagues which ravaged Florence, the villa was used as a lazaretto, housing the ill. Thereafter it remained uninhabited until 1691 when Palmiero Palmieri enlarged and updated the villa in the exuberant baroque taste of the time. Clearly the intervening centuries had brought the family prosperity as Palmiero added the enormous balustraded south terrace, extending it outwards to allow the old road to Fiesole to pass beneath it. He also added the tall front gate posts and the monumental double staircase descending in curving ramps to the lemon garden below. Zocchi's 1744 engraving depicts this space as an oval parterre with a circular pool, central fountain jet, box-hedged swirls and potted lemon trees.

In 1765 the villa entered the Anglo-Florentine community when it was purchased by George, 3rd Earl Cowper. In 1759 the MP for Hertford took a holiday in Florence from which he never returned. Having fallen in love with a married Florentine, he settled, eventually, for a young Englishwoman, Hannah Gore. Unlike many of his compatriots, Cowper was a favourite of Florentine society among whom he freely mixed, organising concerts, contributing to local causes, collecting modern as well as ancient art and joining various learned societies. He was a great friend of the

BELOW *A famous showplace, the villa was subject to the whims of fashion as each owner placed their own stamp on the property. Charles Latham's 1905 photograph shows the courtyard filled with the lush exotic planting of the late Victorian era.*

enlightened ruler Grand Duke Pietro Leopoldo, and used his influence to secure permission for English artists to copy in the Uffizi Gallery. To his compatriots Cowper was an endless source of fascination. Horace Walpole, intrigued that any Englishman would eschew his earldom for 'a pinchpeck principality', described Cowper as 'as great a curiosity as any in the Tuscan collection', while the English Ambassador, Sir Horace Mann, frequently recounted Cowper's brilliant entertainments in his letters home. On Cowper's death the estate remained within the British community when his heirs sold it to a Mary Farhill who later bequeathed it to the Grand Duchess Maria Antonia of Tuscany.

With its rich, romantic history and sylvan setting, it is hardly surprising that the Earl of Crawford and Balcarres would fall in love with the place, purchasing it in 1873 from the Grand Duchess. A noted Italophile,

ABOVE *The elegant double ramp at the Villa Palmieri is one of the garden's most illustrious features; an enclosed loggia built into its base acted as a* limonaia *to over-winter precious citruses from the lemon garden in front.*

Crawford transformed the estate; like Henry Ross at Poggio Gherardo, he planted the hillside behind with exotic trees. More dramatically, he closed the old road to San Domenico which had severed the estate, creating a new road to the east and establishing one of those grand cypress-lined approach roads so beloved of the Anglo-Florentines. Harold Acton reports that after the road was shifted, the Brethren of the Misericordia, who had been accustomed to resting on its verge before continuing their steep ascent to Fiesole, were invited to take their ease in the new garden by the side gate. Not everyone was so easily appeased by the changes however; visiting in 1912 Le Blond noted that the earlier fine gates and approach, with the house standing out boldly above, 'is poorly compensated for by the convenient carriage way which lands visitors at the level of the great court'. Similarly, Lady Paget, recalling an earlier visit, bemoans 'the scent of oranges and lemons [which] was heavy on the air as we passed the Villa Palmieri, not yet spoilt by the ugly new road which now overlooks the grounds'.

The Crawfords enlarged the garden, introducing the rather grandly named 'cactus walk' – a path lined with agaves, a plant which was introduced from the New World in 1520 and could just possibly have featured in the garden's earliest baroque scheme. They also created a parterre below the lemon garden, with distinctive Victorian fan-shaped beds. Later still they added a tennis court and swimming pool; flanked by a summer house with an elegant loggia, the pool was discreet enough to pass as a large reflecting pond, though Le Blond acerbically describes it as 'of not very pleasing design. The same may be said of its fountain.'

Though the Crawfords, in typically English fashion, smothered their walls with roses and filled their parterres with bright bedding plants, they appear to have left the lemon garden untouched. The unlikely survival of this delightful feature through several centuries of keen horticulturists is probably due to its whimsical charm, which appealed equally to Baroque extroverts and English romantics.

After the earl's death in 1880 his widow completed the villa's Anglicisation when, in 1888, she entertained a fellow widow, Queen Victoria. Responding to rumours of the savagery of this outpost of the civilised world, the royal visitor arrived with her own bed, desk, pictures and an entourage of 80 attendants; she also insisted that a special water supply be installed and a dedicated telephone be connected. Recalling the event, Georgina Grahame noted, rather sourly, that many local gardeners were 'temporarily sequestered' in anticipation of the royal visit.

Clearly enchanted by what she saw, the queen remained for more than a month. So successful was the visit that she returned for a second stay in 1893. Lady Paget recounts that the tramontana wind blew throughout the visit, chasing away much-needed rain. Attributing this misfortune to the royal presence rather than their

ABOVE *Built in the grounds of the Villa Palmieri, the Villa Schifanoia was restored to its Renaissance splendour in the 1930s with a classical garden of parterres, fountains, statuary and pools.*

wanton deforestation, the locals prayed for the visitor to leave. During the drought, 'Everyone fell ill through the want of moisture in the air', and Paget herself spent ten francs a day buying water. Remarkably, as the royal train pulled out of the station on 11 April 1893, the precious rains began and continued for a full fortnight.

On Lady Crawford's death in 1907 the villa began its American incarnation when it was purchased by a Mr Ellsworth. Le Blond reports that Mr Ellsworth 'has greatly improved the gardens'. The architect George Elgood, however, complained that the main loggia had been glazed, a fate which befell many Tuscan villas under Anglo-Florentine ownership. While depriving the arcade of its deep shadows, this also undermined the original purpose of the space, turning what had been a subtle link between dwelling and garden into a mundane room.

The American architect, Harold Eberlein, visiting in 1922, was more impressed. While descrying the polychrome decorations, stucco relief and ornamentation of the villa's façade he expresses unqualified admiration for the balustraded terrace with its distinctive curved ramps descending to the parterre below. Indeed, he concludes with the obsequious observation that the recent restoration had been done with such sympathy that 'one may well be thankful that this historic spot has fallen into such intelligent and reverent ownership'.

Visiting several years later Rose Nichols agrees with her compatriot, though she does observe that a vast improvement could be made by replacing the palms with cypresses. Later Nichols mentions that the curved staircase descends 'to a flowery orchard', revealing that the lowest parterre had lost any vestige of its original for-mality. More interestingly, she suggests that the fountain basin at its centre was of Moorish design. Oddly enough, Harold Acton recalls his parents sporting costumes by Poiret to a masked ball at the villa based on a Persian theme. Clearly the fashion for exoticism inspired by Diaghilev and the Ballets Russes extended as far as Florence in those halcyon days before the Second World War.

Further up the Via Boccaccio towards San Domenico is an elegant dwelling, the Villa Schifanoia. Drawing its name from the early Palmieri history, many believe the villa itself was once a *villino* on the Palmieri estate. In the 1930s the villa was purchased by Myron Taylor, the American ambassador to the Vatican during the pontificate of Pius XII. Using the villa to house his collection of classical art, Taylor restored the gardens in the modern Renaissance style pioneered by Cecil Pinsent. Here high hedges enclose box-edged parterres, austerely ornamented with statues, fountains and pools.

Today the villa is owned by the European University but visitors approaching along the quiet rural road cannot help but recall that path along which Boccaccio's protagonists walked seven centuries earlier: 'conducted by the musicall notes of sweete singing Nightingales and infinite other pretty Birds beside, riding in a tract not much frequented, but richly abounding with faire hearbes and flowres...'.

RIGHT *The swimming pool created by the Crawfords in the late nineteenth century. During her long stay at the villa Queen Victoria took tea each afternoon in the loggia overlooking the pool.*

4

A taste for exotica
SIR FREDERICK STIBBERT'S villa

ABOVE *Stibbert delighted in dressing up, often drawing on his vast collection of European, Oriental and Islamic armour. The grand hall in his villa contained models of fourteen mounted medieval knights and fourteen foot soldiers all sporting authentic arms and armour.*

OPPOSITE *With the help of the architect Giuseppe Poggi, Stibbert removed the nineteenth-century flower beds surrounding his villa and created an eccentric landscape park, at the heart of which stands an artificial lake with an Egyptian temple at its side.*

SIR FREDERICK STIBBERT (1838–1906) exemplifies the early Anglo-Florentine taste for exotica. Inspired by Florentine ornament, imbued with Victorian eclecticism and given to restless peregrinations, this acquisitive exile assembled an extraordinary estate unconstrained by the historicism of later generations. Stibbert's garden was laid out like an eighteenth-century English landscape park, embellished with nineteenth-century gardenesque features and overlaid with early twentieth-century Art Nouveau sensuality.

Frederick Stibbert was born in Florence where his grandfather retired, having scaled the colonial service to become Governor of Bengal only to be shunned by the establishment on his return to England. Stibbert's father married a Florentine woman and, as their only son, Frederick was duly educated at Harrow then Cambridge. Though his father died while he was a child leaving him independently wealthy, Sibbert joined Garibaldi's army and fought in the Trentino campaign. Over the years he developed a taste for military paraphernalia, and stoked, perhaps, by colonial nostalgia, used the family fortune to help him amass a magnificent collection of armour ranging from Ottoman scimitars to French bayonets, Etruscan helmets to Indian weaponry.

When his acquisitions spilled beyond his sixteenth-century villa, Stibbert purchased the neighbouring nineteenth-century country house, joining the two to create a sixty-four room mansion equipped with all the features essential to an English gentleman, including map room, ballroom, billiard room, music room, smoking room and library. Here William Morris wallpaper, Pre-Raphaelite stained glass, oriental porcelains, Murano chandeliers and Flemish tapestries provided a background for his collection of Dutch and early Renaissance paintings. Here too Stibbert housed the armour, arms and costumes that he donned for the celebrated re-enactments in which the host himself starred as medieval knight, Egyptian god or Highland chieftain.

Stibbert's garden evolved just as capriciously as his villa. While Acton dismissed it as 'quaint' and 'histrionic-historical', recent scholars have hailed it as a rare example of middle-class Victorian landscape style. Though the setting has been extensively developed since Susan and Joanna Horner, in their 1873 *Walks in Florence*, described a view of 'hill and valley richly cultivated', the garden itself, neglected through the twentieth century, remains much as Stibbert left it. In 1905 Latham enthused: 'Driving up the slopes, the attention is caught every moment by some interesting piece of stonework….Here is a little shrine of the renaissance, there a fine old carved well-head.' While the villa is now accessed from above, the car park conveys some of the tantalising eclecticism of the original approach, being flanked by a Moorish pavilion implausibly housing a naked Venus.

Stibbert's famous Gothic terrace – a collection of thir-teenth-century columns ranged round a Venetian wellhead – has long-since disappeared, but the air of architectural salvage remains. The villa's external walls bristle with crests, shields, coats of arms and other archaeological accretions. Faded frescoes beneath the turret's loggia depict the twelfth-century Roman adventurer, Captain Ugo, who laid waste to the surrounding Montughi hillside before settling at its apex and giving the slope his name. The terrace in front holds Roman sarcophagi, while parkland beyond descends through meadow and woodland, to the valley below. Here grottoes, oil jars, statues and sundry relics litter the land-scape, gravel paths meander through bamboos, bananas, palms and other exotica, while an avenue lined with antique busts presents a more traditional touch.

At the heart of this assemblage sits a small lake sur-rounded by cypress, cedars and other gloomy conifers that were fashionable in the late nineteenth century. A small island hosts a solitary swamp cypress, but the focal point, at the head of the water, is an Egyptian temple. This may well have been inspired by Masonic initiation ceremonies as Stibbert was a member of La Concordia, Italy's oldest and most powerful Masonic lodge. Guarded by pairs of Theban sphinxes, crouching lions and carved priests, the temple is reputed to house an authentic Egyptian priestess mummy.

Stibbert's whimsy was tolerated as English eccentricity and the visiting Queen Victoria happily sketched in his now defunct Gothic terrace. On his death, childless and unmarried, Stibbert bequeathed his estate to the British Government – an attempt, perhaps, to gain the recognition denied his grandfather. The grounds soon sunk into neglect, acquiring the romantic dilapidation so beloved of English horticulturists, and for many years the British Council held official receptions in their midst. Eventually the estate passed to the city of Florence and today it is run as a vibrant museum though the gardens retain their lugubrious air.

As Stibbert's was essentially an urban garden, one cannot help wondering what marvels he might have created had he been born a generation later and submitted to the scholarly historicism of Vernon Lee, Edith Wharton, Bernard Berenson, Harold Acton et al. Yet, while Stibbert epitomises the early Anglo-Florentine ignorance of – and lack of interest in – historically appropriate styles, his creation is not so different from that quintessential Italian estate, the Villa Borghese. Richard Lassel's 1670s *Voyage of Italy*, describes the Borghese gardens as containing:

ABOVE *Even the exterior of Stibbert's villa bristled with architectural salvage, boasting everything from iron torch holders to stone plaques, crests and shields.*

> walks, both open and close, Fish-Ponds, vast Cages for Birds, thickets of Trees, store of Fountains, a Park of Deer, a world of Fruit-trees, Statues of all sizes, Banquetting places, Grotta's, Wetting Sports, and a stately Pallace adorned with many rare statues….The Wall of the House is overcrusted with a world of *Anticallie* or old Marble-pieces of antiquity….Entring into the house, I saw divers Rooms full of curiosities…

This catalogue suggests that Stibbert's eclectic assemblage was not without precedent in Italian horticulture.

Stibbert's sister, Sofronia, was an equally committed, if less eccentric, horticulturist. Having married the Count Alessio Pandolfini, she revived the gardens of the family's historic Palazzo Pandolfini. The only Tuscan villa known to have been designed by Raphael, this handsome palazzo was built on the northeastern edge of the city at a time when gentlemen left the cramped urban centres to create suburban dwellings where they could enjoy rural life without sacrificing metropolitan pleasures. Though Florence has expanded to engulf the estate, the extensive grounds attest to that sixteenth-century passion for cultivating exotic plants in classical settings.

Following the fashion of the time, the countess extended winter interest in her gardens with collections of prize-winning camellias and rare cinerarias. Developed by Britain's royal gardeners in the late eighteenth century, cineraria was valued by the Victorians for its ability to flower through frost-free winters. Though Edith Wharton despised the inauthentic burst of colour it gave to many Florentine gardens, it remains a favourite to this day. The villa itself, still owned by the family, is not open to the public, though its gardens can be glimpsed from the palace gates on the Via San Gallo.

BELOW *Stibbert's famous gothic terrace: a Venetian wellhead surrounded by a fourteenth-century stone colonnade, embellished with exotic banana plants.*

5
A Pre-Raphaelite paradise
LADY PAGET'S Torre di Bellosguardo

ONE OF THE LEAST LIKELY, but most prominent, of the Anglo-Florentine garden makers was the Saxon princess, Walburga Helena de Hohenthal, known to her friends as Wally, and to history as Walburga, Lady Paget (1839–1929). Despite her German birth, Paget was the unchallenged doyenne of the expatriate community by virtue of her marriage, in 1860, to Sir Augustus Berkeley Paget, British ambassador, variously, to Copenhagen, Vienna, Portugal, Florence and Rome, whom the American writer Mabel Luhan dismissed as 'greatly her inferior as a human being'.

Paget first saw Florence in 1865 when her husband was posted as ambassador to the newly unified country. The official residence was in such poor condition that she declared it uninhabitable, eventually settling herself and her three children in the Palazzo Orlandini, an elegant early nineteenth-century building with a large garden near the Duomo. Despite having to retreat to the coast periodically when cholera ravaged the city, Paget loved her first sojourn in Florence, recalling later in old age:

> There is a refinement, an understanding, an intelligence about everything there which keeps the mind always on the alert. The air to me was like champagne and the interest of awakening to a new life in art and beauty was almost akin to pain, for I feared no life could be long enough to take it all in.

When, in 1870, the capital moved to Rome, Paget was so distraught at the thought of leaving that she almost refused to go. On her eventual arrival in the city, Paget was charged with finding and furnishing a residence suitable for the English ambassador as her husband was immediately called to London. Although she was drawn to the Villa Farnese, its priestly owners refused to rent it to representatives of a protestant country, and so eventually she settled on the Villa Torlonia, a large estate at the edge of the city surrounded with vineyards and ancient monuments.

Seven years later Paget had to leave Italy when her husband was posted to Vienna, but when he retired to England in 1887, Paget returned to her beloved Florence. After renting the Villa Caprini in Fiesole for several years, in 1893 she purchased the medieval Torre di Bellosguardo south of the city.

Here Paget retreated from diplomatic and spousal duties, restoring her villa and creating an informal garden around it. Acknowledging that her refusal to accompany her husband through the English season was unconventional, to say the least, she explained: 'I had wasted so much time in former years in paying visits, and the empty and artificial life which one is obliged to lead was so utterly distasteful to me that I could not make up my mind to go on with it.'

In the eight volumes of her diaries Paget describes the court life of *fin de siècle* Europe, recording deaths, suicides, scandals, intrigues, *coups d'état*, balls, concerts and visits, revealing through her lively prose the unconscious prejudices of her class. Mabel Luhan suggests that Paget settled in Italy because British quarantine laws prevented her from repatriating the beloved, velvet-brown dachshunds given to her by Elizabeth Barrett Browning's son, Pen. It is unlikely however that this solitary, free spirit could have settled within the restrictive structures of English society. In 1893, during a visit to London, she confides to her diary: 'I long for the pure air of my mountain-top, Florence spread out at my feet, and peace around me', before adding, 'spoke to the Princess of Wales at the Palace Concert'.

Despite her unorthodox lifestyle, Paget maintained strict, if idiosyncratic, social rules, observing that though she never visits, her own Friday 'at homes' are always mobbed:

> Society here seems quite changed since my time. In those days very few women went out into society, but masses of men. The women who appeared were nearly all young and pretty, but not very correct….Now the young women of Florence are perfectly correct; they think of nothing but their children; they only wear Worth gowns, they are infinitely dull, and seem to have frightened all the men away.

The reference to Worth gowns might refer to Ouida or Lady Sybil Cutting, both of whom patronised the famous French designer.

After her husband's death in 1897 Paget retreated increasingly to her villa, where she held court in home-made gothic gowns, taught hygiene to the local children, and

ABOVE *Paget campaigned to preserve the city's medieval features; after reporting that the sparrows of Santa Maria Nuova died, 'having dined on a plate of plague-broth which had been put on the windowsill', her diary for December 1896 records a plan to pull down some ancient dwellings: ' Nominally a sanitary measure but in reality a camorra of architects and builders who have got the weak backed Syndic into their hands…'.*

lent her name to various campaigns to halt the destruction of medieval Florence. Indeed, the widespread demolition of the city's ancient structures galvanized the foreign community as little else could do; Vernon Lee wrote impassioned reports to *The Times* in London, while Augustus Hare, in his popular guide, *Florence*, publicly lamented the pulling down of the Mercato Vecchio by an 'ignorant and short sighted Municipality'. Claiming that 'every wall, every stone, recorded a page of Florentine history' he suggested that if the quarter had simply been cleaned and restored, it could have presented a perfect example of medieval architecture.

When not taken up with conservation activities Paget pursued theosophy, spiritualism, vegetarianism and a dizzying whirl of social obligations. Nonetheless while her diaries show an understanding of contemporary politics, her passion was clearly her garden. The tower at the heart of her estate was built at the beginning of the fourteenth century by the aristocrat, Guido Cavalcanti – a respected poet and friend of Dante. Clearly proud of this latter detail Paget repeats it throughout her memoirs, as though to balance the association with Boccaccio brandished by her fellow expatriates at the villas I Tatti, Poggio Gherardo and Il Palmieri north of the city. Listing the villa's other illustrious owners as the Capponis, the Medici and Cosimo's favourite

BELOW *Although houses were cheap to buy they were impossible to heat as the massive stone walls and large, deep windows kept interiors permanently cold and damp. Like many expatriates Paget transformed her loggia into a snug winter sitting room by glazing the windows and adding a large fireplace.*

architect Michelozzi, Paget also asserts that Byron's ill-fated lover Claire Clairemont and Shelley's wife Mary were earlier inhabitants and that her house inspired Elizabeth Barrett Browning's 1855 *Aurora Leigh* – although the same distinction is claimed, more plausibly, by the nearby Villa Brichieri-Colombi where Barrett Browning frequently visited her friend, the writer, Isa Blagden.

While Torre di Bellosguardo started as a defensive tower, over the centuries new wings were added and embellished to create what Luhan described as 'a beautiful old villa that [Paget] restored and filled with her romantic personality'. Paget also left her mark on the fabric of the villa. Like many expatriates she soon discovered that the high ceilinged, thick walled rooms which provided such relief in the airless Florentine summers were also gaunt, barren and impossible to heat through the long damp winters. Rising to the challenge, however, Paget committed the architectural heresy of glazing her loggia to create a sun-warmed winter sitting room, then multiplied her comfort by adding a fireplace – much more efficient than the short, black, tin stoves, known to the Anglo-Florentines as 'little pigs'.

Cosily settled in her loggia the indomitable Paget braved snowstorms, blocked roads, frozen water and sparse food supplies, cheerfully awaiting the February violets, aconites, gillyflowers and the tiny narcissus which the Italians called *tazzette*.

Despite such compensations, many travellers seduced by the fantasy of Florence's beneficial climate, were shocked to discover the brutal winters. Paget herself frequently berated the Italians for their irresponsible tree-felling which left no shelter from the biting *tramontana* winds. In 1929 the garden writer Rose Nichols, noting that Pietro Crescenzi's fourteenth-century *De Agricultura* recommends palms for evergreen adornment, wryly observed: 'even at this early date, long before the hotel-keepers on the Riviera thought of using it to deceive people as to the mild winter climate there, the tropical palm had begun to find its way to Italy'. More forcefully, in her 1859 *Life in Tuscany* the American traveller Mabel Sharman Crawford cursed, 'oh poets and novel writers! Great is the responsibility resting on your heads for having fostered the huge illusion which generally prevails with regard to the blessedness of an Italian winter clime.'

While charting the transformation of her stable yard from 'a howling wilderness ravined by drains' to a lavish if casual paradise, Paget's diaries provide a fascinating picture of the better-known gardens of the time. She dismisses the richly iconographical Villa Lante as 'a small Versailles embowered in leafy Etrurian shades'. At the Villa Farnese she extols the campagna 'like shot silk', describing the garden as desolate but still beautiful, with roses 'twined around the tall Hermes, which stood in rows along the terrace paths now hiding and then again giving glimpses of the blue Apennines'. She calls Marlia 'fresh and green as Switzerland, with rushing streams and tall walnut and chestnut trees', but barely mentions the gardens except to note the wooded amphitheatre behind the villa and the high fountain in the lawn in front. Of the Villa Cetinale she merely observes that it stands 'in an amphitheatre of ilex-covered terraces. A fine avenue, with one of the rare Italian ghosts, leads up to it.' Even that perennial favourite, the Villa Gamberaia, Paget describes as 'a dream'; ignoring its formal qualities and reducing its baroque design to 'a most poetic place, so retired and so beautiful'.

Deploring the fashion for exotica, she complained, after a visit to the South of France, that the only flowers to be seen were in the gardens of the rich,

> who bed out their roses, wisterias and laburnums and put them back into houses for the night....Cannes I think detestable; it is a long string of villas built by millionaires. They all spend enormous sums in keeping up sub-tropical vegetation, beds of specimen flowers, artificial lawns which have to be re-sown every year. Everything about these gardens reeks of money.

Not surprisingly, she also dismisses the grand gardens of the Italian lakes, detecting 'something meretricious in it all after the sober lines of the Tuscan hills and the sombre tones of the *campagna*'.

LEFT *Paget preferred a romantic Pre-Raphaelite tangle to the crisp geometry of classical Renaissance horticulture.*

ABOVE *The aptly named village of Bellosguardo encompasses within its 'beautiful view' the whole of Florence, with Brunelleschi's iconic Duomo and Giotto's elegant Campanile highlighted against the backdrop of the surrounding hills.*

In keeping with the austere spirit of her chosen landscape, Paget's horticultural tastes combined gothic fantasy with an English love of nature, shaped no doubt by her friends William and Evelyn De Morgan and the Burne-Joneses. Her bedroom window, grilled in the medieval fashion, was 'hung with Spanish jessamine' – more Pre-Raphaelite than Tuscan vernacular. Indeed Paget self-consciously evokes artists when describing her garden, noting her red roses 'against the Perugino sky', her rose bower 'like an Alma Tadema' and her grass walks carpeted with buttercups and daisies 'fit for Fra Angelico's angels to tread'.

Although the centre of Florence was only a few miles away, Paget emphasised the rural aspect of her estate. While she fails to describe the layout or planting, her diary gives an impression of cottagey profusion and she frequently extols the intoxicating scent of lemon trees, nicotiana, roses, lilies and honeysuckle. The blurry photographs which dot her memoirs reveal wild flower strewn lawns, baroque walls laced with greenery and olive groves studded with irises. When Queen Victoria – whom she befriended while helping to arrange the marriage of the Prince of Wales to a Danish princess – came to visit on Good Friday 1893, Paget records simply that they took 'a quiet stroll in the *podere*', suggesting that the farmyard was the main horticultural feature.

ABOVE *The chatelaine posing under the wisteria in one of her flowing, hand-made robes.*

Advancing age and impeccable class notwithstanding, Paget bemused her Italian neighbours by working in the grounds. Rising at dawn, she would go straight to the garden to dig, paint, construct paths and even break stones for gravel. Equally eccentrically, she expected her guests to take their turn, noting of Lord Lamington, the recently appointed Governor of Queensland, 'Wallace is excellent, simple and true; he weeded a great many baskets of groundsel'.

Despite her rather fey, privileged lifestyle, Paget was one of the few expatriates to question the effect of her presence on the host country. In 1913, amid rumours of impending war, the septuagenarian reluctantly returned to England. In 1924, writing the prelude to her memoirs, she noted: 'When I first came to Italy in the later sixties there was much of the ancient simplicity, sobriety and love of work and beauty in the nation.' Returning, years later, she was struck by the degradation to which the country had sunk, a state she attributes to 'the great influx of foreigners', whose money brought materialism while destroying 'the native austerity and gaiety'.

Impoverishment rather than materialism is more likely the cause of the discontent; by 1924 Italy had been bankrupted by the First World War. Amid rising unemployment people began demanding the break-up of large estates so land could be redistributed to returning soldiers. Like the wealthier Italian peasants and land-owners, Italy's expatriates were frightened by the situation. In 1920 the government's threat to raise income taxes and nationalise power and fuel provoked a general strike; the following year riots in Florence left several people dead and hundreds wounded. In 1922, promising an organised, law-abiding party, Benito Mussolini, at thirty nine, was voted the youngest prime minister in Italian history.

From the vantage point of her English dower house, Paget hailed the new leader as 'courageous and single-minded'. Like many foreigners, she was seduced by his claim to have saved the country from Communism. While few expatriates still living in the country were so effusive in their praise, most were prepared to tolerate

Mussolini, appeased by his pro-capitalist stance, imposition of order, abolition of state bureaucracy, grand building programme and much vaunted ability to make the trains run on time. Happily Paget did not live to see the error of her judgement. In 1929, while dozing by the fire at Unlawater House in Newnham-on-Severn, her newspaper caught fire. Her butler managed to rip off her skirts before she was burned, but the nonagenarian died in hospital several hours later – an event which was reported in *Time* magazine.

In 1913 Paget's beloved Bellosguardo had been bought by an Austrian aristocrat, Baroness Marion von Hornstein, grandmother to the present owners. A spirited cosmopolitan separated from her husband, von Hornstein, like Paget, lived alone in the villa. When her fortunes were devastated by the First World War, she maintained the estate by taking in paying guests, among the more illustrious of which was Rupert, Crown Prince of Bavaria, successor to the Jacobite throne. Like his ancestor Bonnie Prince Charlie, Rupert sought refuge in Florence, although in his case it was the Germans rather than the English he was fleeing. As with most grand villas, Bellosguardo was commandeered during the Second World War, first by the local German command and later by the Allies.

In the 1950s when high taxes and high wages made it impossible to maintain such a large private residence, the estate was rented out to American schools, among them the prestigious women's arts college, Sarah Lawrence. In the 1970s the Franchettis, who had been working in advertising in America, returned to their native Italy and took over the estate, discreetly transforming it into the exclusive hilltop hotel which it remains today.

RIGHT *Paget was particularly proud of her battlemented tower; such features attested to the centuries of conflict in which these romantic villas were steeped.*

George S. Elgood 1902

6
A Tuscan flower garden
GEORGINA GRAHAME'S English borders

ABOVE *Although tantalisingly secretive about her personal identity, Grahame recounts her horticultural activities in* In a Tuscan Garden *(1902), followed seven years later by* Under Petraia *which describes creating a second home in Tuscany after her eviction from the first.*

OPPOSITE *George Elgood,* A Florentine Terrace *(detail), 1904. Unable to relinquish the prospect of flowers many Anglo-Florentines filled their Tuscan villas with potted plants which required less water than ground plants and could be moved to shade when necessary.*

ALTHOUGH IT WAS NEVER IDENTIFIED and has probably long since disappeared, one of the most intriguing of the Anglo-Florentine projects was the garden created by the enigmatic Georgina Grahame in the hills above Florence. While few of the Anglo-Florentines could conceive of a garden entirely devoid of flora, many accepted the limitations of the climate and planted their flowers in pots which could be easily watered or moved into shade. Some, however, challenged the existing conditions and bullied the Tuscan earth to bring forth English-style lawns and floral borders. The prime exemplar of this sort of horticultural arrogance is the indomitable Georgina Grahame who recorded her experience in her 1902 *In A Tuscan Garden*.

With discretion common to her gender and class Grahame published anonymously and as she does not figure in other memoirs of the community, the only impression we have of her is what she reveals in her book. A passing reference to her native Eskdale, plus the preponderance of Scots staff, friends and visitors reveal her origins in Northern England. There is a casual mention of a son and daughter, while her husband, the 'Absentee', appears to have been either a diplomat or a spy as he spent most of his time in a caravanserai in Constantinople or disappearing off to distant parts 'where his gift of tongues was to be utilized for the good of his country'.

Despite her deliberate obfuscations Grahame was clearly part of the expatriate community as she refers to the dreaded 'at home day' – 'that scourge of the British resident in Italy', before conceding that it does, at least, inspire one's gardener to tidy the grounds. She also mourns the passing of the community's early members, those 'learned and cultivated American diplomatists, in whose hospitable villa were to be met the people best worth knowing of all nationalities', and while she refuses to name the characters who feature in her account, she does make a clear reference to Janet Ross, whom she describes as 'the only surviving notability of that period', before commenting, contemptuously, on Ross' commercial activities.

Though Grahame has been condemned by modern historians as priggish and jingoistic, her book reveals an Anglo-Florentine approach which was common before Wharton enlightened the public as to the flowerless state of classical Italian horticulture. In a chapter entitled, 'Italian Gardens Old and Modern', Grahame explains:

> Most of us have come under the spell of the charm of the old gardens…with their groves of cypress and ilex trees, their fountains and their statuary, all recalling the splendour of a bygone past – delightful places in which to dream away the hot hours of the summer afternoon…[but] none of these are gardens in the English sense of the word, a place in which to plant and cultivate the flowers we love best.

In a later chapter she adds, 'The well-ordered English garden, beloved of its owners, and cultivated by them and their forefathers for generations, is not to be met with in Italy.'

Certainly, in nineteenth-century Italy, flowers were grown primarily as a commercial crop, and usually for export; most Italians felt cut flowers were unhealthy indoors so the domestic flower market was limited to wreaths and funeral decorations. Grahame's bewildered staff could not understand why she would leave her own flowers in the ground just for the pleasure of looking at them, while wasting good money buying cut flowers from the market: 'A Tuscan garden is not a thing of beauty or to be cultivated for pleasure; it is a commercial asset.' Indeed her book begins with a lengthy condemnation of both Italy and the Anglo-Florentine fantasy: 'Old Italian villas, about which so much has been written and to the idea of which so much romance clings, are, as a matter of fact, for the most part, gaunt, barren, hideous structures outside, and conspicuous for every kind of inconvenience within.' She goes on to explain that most villas are divided into flats, and while the ground floor tenants have access to the garden, as it remains the property of the landlord it is usually ignored and neglected. She then recounts how the late King of Wurtemburg, having rented a beautiful old villa, was surprised to discover that he had to pay the gardener for every bunch of violets gathered.

While such contempt for her host country is wearing, Grahame's love of horticulture is palpable, her energy is prodigious and her garden sounds delightful, if misguided. As Grahame tantalisingly refuses to divulge the exact location of her villa, the only record of her garden is that which she offers in her book with its blurry black-and-white photographs. Although long out of print, a copy is duly lodged at the British Institute, where its well-thumbed pages provide a vivid account of a particular style of late nineteenth-century Anglo-Florentine garden-making.

Having settled in Florence in the 1860s she exhibits a peculiarly Victorian combination of gentility, prudery and xenophobia, laced with snobbishness against her own countrymen. Indeed of her fellow Anglo-Florentines she complained,

> In my time…the fashion for English people to inhabit country houses in the neighbourhood of Florence was almost unknown. Here and there an Anglo-Italian settled in Italy for business or other reasons, might own a property on which he would spend a few weeks in summer. But the English in those days had not spread themselves over the face of the land as they have since done.

Setting her story squarely in the Anglo-Florentine tradition, however, Grahame begins by recounting how she visited all manner of unsuitable properties till one afternoon, while walking with her companion – the unnamed female 'Junior Partner' with whom she lives – Grahame stumbles across a noble villa, languishing at the end of the ubiquitous cypress-lined drive. This is the 'once-upon-a-time' of the Anglo-Florentine experience, and the story proceeds to explain how the author explores the overgrown estate and discovers a modest two-storey *villino* in a walled courtyard with a *stanzone* or lemon house attached. Having negotiated a lease with the owner of the property the real story begins as our author heroically restores the place to its former glory, wresting a vibrant garden despite the efforts of wily workers and unscrupulous bureaucrats to thwart her.

In Grahame's case the large Medici villa on to whose land she stumbled had been the country residence of an English Minister at the court of the Grand Dukes

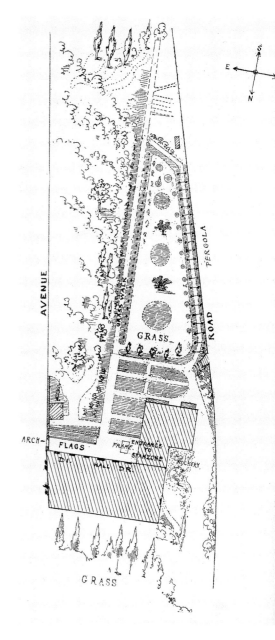

ABOVE *In this remarkably professional sketch, Grahame proudly shows her readers the full extent of her horticultural achievements.*

of Tuscany. It is possible that her house was in the grounds of Careggi, the Medici villa north of the city which Lord Holland rented in 1845 while acting as English ambassador and which, to this day, is surrounded by an unusual English-style park. To her delight, the ambassador had placed his coat of arms over the main entrance, cloaked the villa walls in roses and imposed his taste upon the grounds in the form of a large, landscape park filled with ilexes, conifers, tulip trees and catalpas. To the north was Fiesole, 'the old Etruscan mother city', to the east were the Vallombrosa hills and just below, 'veiled in the misty light of the hot June sun' were the domes and spires of Florence with the Apennines rising beyond to the south. From the park a walk led to the garden proper, 'now, alas, in a fearful state of decadence'… as such gardens always were.

Since large expanses of parkland were unusual in Tuscany's hilly terrain, it was this feature which finally convinced Grahame. Taking a lease on the neglected *villino*, she employed a Scottish architect to oversee the restorations, removing walls, adding windows, supplementing the two open fireplaces with efficient stoves and installing servant bells in every room before moving in with her companion, her Scottish maid and a local housekeeper. The interior walls were stencilled with designs copied from Italian brocades, and furniture was shipped from London. Before a porter's lodge was built she kept her silver behind closed doors but later, with the security of locked gates and a vigilant guard, she proudly displayed choice bits of antique English silver on the dining room shelves.

Like many expatriates, Grahame imported domestic staff to protect herself from daily contact with the local people. A few decades earlier Elizabeth Barrett Browning had eloped to Italy, taking along her London maid, the faithful 'Wilson', who soon abandoned her mistress to marry an Italian manservant. Such situations were not unusual as both Dickens and Ruskin lost their English domestics to Italian husbands during extended stays in the city. Intermarriage was also common among the highest classes where impecunious Italian nobles eagerly exchanged their titles for large American dowries; unfortunately, however, as the novels of Henry James and E.M. Forster suggest, the resulting unions tended to be marked by misunderstanding more often than joy.

Despite the security of her Scottish maid, Grahame was unable to entice a Scottish, or even an English cook to oversee her kitchen. Eventually, reluctantly, she hired a local woman. She was also forced, reluctantly, to hire local garden staff and devotes a whole chapter to the horrors of Tuscan servants. Many foreigners were similarly in thrall to their employees, unable to function without them, but resentful of their presence. This antagonistic relationship became particularly strained in the 1920s when Mussolini introduced labour laws forbidding foreigners from firing an Italian employee without huge compensation. Such antagonism was not confined to the Fascist era however. In 1897 Lady Paget dismissed a servant with the appropriate fifteen day warning; when she refused his unlawful demand for money he took her to court. Although she won the case, the man disappeared, leaving her to pay the costs. Paget concludes her account of the episode: 'This is an experience which most foreigners living in Italy will be able to confirm.' Grahame recounts similar conflicts with staff and describes a particularly unpleasant incident when a cook whom she refused to employ later sued her for breach of contract. Such petty frustrations, however, were a small price to pay for the prospect of a villa, garden and a view of the Tuscan hills.

In the late nineteenth century, the Tuscans had little interest in gardens as the term was understood by the English and American expatriates. Villas had been built on

BELOW *The old stone archway which Grahame gated to prevent local peasants from walking past her front door on a short cut to other parts of the estate.*

hilltops for the encompassing views, and by the time the Anglo-Florentines arrived, views were about all that was left of them. Constance Fenimore Woolson extolled the view from her rented apartment in Bellosguardo's Villa Brichieri-Colombi, claiming 'it commands not only the "sweet Val d'Arno" as Ruskin calls it, but all Florence with its domes and towers'. Her short story, *Dorothy*, describes the garden itself:

> when one ceases to look at the view – if one ever does cease – one perceives that the nook has no formal flower-beds; grass, dotted with the pink daisies of Italy, stretches from the house walls to the edge; here and there are rose-bushes, pomegranates, oleanders and laurel, but all are half wild.

In his 1875 *Roderick Hudson* Henry James, inspired by the neighbouring Villa Castellani, evokes a similar scene of ragged charm: a strip of grass bounded by a wall, screened by orange blossoms and fig trees, 'and over the low parapet the soft grave Tuscan landscape kept you company'. The English writer known as Ouida used her own Villa Farinola as a template for the dwelling in her 1873 novel *Pascarel*, noting:

> where these old villas stand on their pale olive slopes, those who are strange to them see only the peeling plaster, the discoloured stones, the desolate courts, the grass-grown flags, broken statues, the straying vines, the look of loneliness and decay. But those who know them well…learn the infinite charm of those vast silent halls, of those endless echoing corridors and cloisters, of those wide wind-swept sunbathed chambers, of those shadowy loggie where the rose-flow of the oleander bursts in the dimness of the arches…

Having spent several seasons seeking a villa to settle in, the American writer Mabel Dodge Luhan was less enchanted by crumbling walls and picturesque neglect; in her memoirs she complains that the typical garden of the time was a dreary, flowerless plot smelling of box, flanked with unkempt bushes, leading to a damp stone bench. From such inauspicious material the Anglo-Florentine garden was wrought.

As Grahame warns in her book, the first thing any Anglo-Florentine garden maker learned was that horticultural knowledge they brought from home was virtually useless. Good soil, such as that the English took for granted, did not exist in Tuscany and Grahame explains that the local earth is suited only to vines and tea roses – she might also have added peonies and lilies.

While labour was cheap, fuel was not, and it was the landlord's responsibility to supply the wood to heat the greenhouse which sheltered the citrus, orchids, bulbs and tender exotics through the winter. Water was another valuable commodity. In the absence of wells or springs, water was collected and stored in underground brick chambers. When Grahame rented the *villino* she had never had to consider water consumption and was lulled into a false sense of security by the large house cistern and two garden cisterns. While these may have supplied the needs of the average Italian family, they were unable to satisfy the English penchant for daily baths and green gardens. Her contract allowed her to supplement her domestic needs with water from the main villa, but she was often forced to purchase extra water for the garden. This would be delivered, at great expense in wooden barrels which had to be hand-carried over long distances. Grahame used this water on her pot-plants through the hot Tuscan summers, and though she was ruthless with the shrubs, leaving them to expire in the ground, when the peonies or Japanese anemones showed signs of distress she

BELOW *Grahame's prized grass walk was edged with crocuses, of which she claimed: 'I know of nothing among spring flowers that gives the same amount of beauty at so small a cost.'*

ABOVE *While the Renaissance style called for clean architectural lines, Grahame, like many Anglo-Florentines, embellished her villa with climbers and flanking flower beds.*

usually relented and spared them a drop. This scarcity of water forced Tuscan gardeners to improvise, and Grahame triumphantly reports that after much trial and error she has discovered that ivy-leafed pelargonium can withstand 'any amount of heat and drought'.

Fertiliser was a further expense; those with no stable of their own were forced to purchase manure at considerable cost. The local name for fertilising dung was *pecorino* since it was usually comprised of sheep's droppings, often administered as a liquid to encourage tender shrubs to flower. Grahame supplemented this with cow dung for her roses, while her prized green lawn was given an annual sprinkling of wood ash, carefully saved from the winter fires and stored in the cellars beneath the *stanzone*.

To minimise the cost of fertiliser most gardeners made compost from garden refuse, kitchen waste and wood ash, though Grahame reports that having finally convinced the chimney sweep to save the soot for her beloved carnations she discovered that a rival raised superb examples on nothing more than a daily dose of coffee grounds. She also complains of the expense of the various different types of earth which had to be purchased in large quantities for the annual repotting of tender specimens.

Finding competent, reliable help was a major problem for Anglo-Florentine garden makers, exacerbated, no doubt, by the fact that there was often no common language between employer and employee. Gardeners were hired on the ancient *mezzadria* system, similar to that used by tenant farmers. Under this scheme the owner would provide land, green-house, fuel, plant material and fertiliser while the gardener often worked for free in exchange for the right to sell surplus produce. Another common arrangement was for the gardener to receive a small wage and half the profits from any sales of plants or vegetables. Ever suspicious of her Italian employees, Grahame ensured against cheating on the part of her gardener by hiring an accountant to estimate probable yields before the final settling up.

Obtaining plants was another trial. While the local nurseries did not carry the flowers Grahame required, she concedes that they stocked many beautiful and inexpensive flowering shrubs which were only just beginning to be introduced to England. While she complains that the local nurserymen are 'very unscientific', she does allow that they are industrious and hardworking. In attempting to furnish her garden Grahame discovered that imports were of limited use as English or American seeds rarely survived the heavy Tuscan soil. Cuttings were the major source of plant material, though even this practice had to be adapted to local conditions; it took Grahame several years to work out that while the English strike chrysanthemum cuttings in late autumn to ensure flowers the following November, in Tuscany cuttings taken in February will provide flourishing plants in just six months. She also recounts her difficulty in obtaining the Scotch briar roses whose scent she particularly favoured; after the local nursery's specimens died she tried a Belgian firm with little success before eventually discovering the fortunate Monsieur Guillôt from Lyon who thereafter fulfilled all her manifold fantasies. Her only problem then was finding in Mr Guillôt's catalogue the equivalent of the roses named in *The Garden* and *Country Life*.

In the custom of the region, Grahame's dwelling was shielded to the north by a dense windbreak of firs; mindful of the bitter winters she left this evergreen barrier, but planted the meadow in front with fruit trees, flowering shrubs and wild flowers, succeeded by nasturtiums ranging in colour from the pale La Pearle to the deepest orange-black. The garden proper lay to the southwest, and it is here that Grahame revealed her horticultural prowess. This inner sanctum was reached via tall brick piers supporting terracotta vases. Erecting a wooden gate to keep out the *contadino* who had made a shortcut past her house, Grahame embellished the gate with a series of overhead wires to create a scented arch of roses and jasmine. Conveniently, the courtyard within was bare earth rather than the usual paving, allowing her to create beds for periwinkles, roses, honeysuckles and violets, all of which were transferred to pots in autumn to make space for the freesias she required for her winter table.

Laid out in the form of a Latin cross, her garden had a flagstone walk lying the length of the house with a cross axis leading to a picturesque trellis-work arbour, surmounted by a huge iron dome and wreathed in Virginia creeper. At the end of the garden stood the 'invaluable' old acacia tree, beneath which she placed her garden chairs. This dining area was surrounded in spring with ferns, scillas, snowdrops and yellow primroses giving way, in summer, to decorative foliage plants and large terracotta pots of azaleas whose delicate flowers were shaded by the spreading tree.

To the horror of her Italian gardener – '*It was a belbosco signora*' – Grahame thinned out the boundary shrubbery to create a deep flower border. Beside this she installed that perennial English favourite, a long grass walk, 'a better background for shrubs and colour effects than anything else'. This feature was the envy of her compatriots, one of whom, 'the owner of a very superior domain', assured her that her grass walk was worth the whole of his estate including the glasshouses and gardeners.

Elsewhere Grahame placed potted magnolias against the dining room window to scent her evening meals, removed a fine muscatel grapevine to make space for her Banksia roses and smothered the villa walls with climbing plants. While Italians, traditionally, preferred the clean lines of unadorned architecture, their reluctance to cloak their walls in verdure also stemmed from a fear of harbouring snakes and noxious insects. Oblivious to this basic danger, Grahame complains, 'You never see a creeper of any kind planted against their walls to soften their staring outline, and they have a desolate forlorn look, in contrast to our lovely English houses.'

In time Grahame also planted exotics in the shelter of her lemon house and added further flower beds and a shrub border. Among her most successful additions were Bengal roses; indeed she planted a long hedge of these vigorous, shrubby Chinese roses along the length of the garden to blossom in both spring and autumn with a mass of scented flowers. Beneath the roses she created a wide belt of white pinks and behind it, for spring colour, a double row of 400 yellow tulips. The scent in this region must have been intoxicating as Grahame planted the far side of the hedge with Madonna lilies alternating with peonies 'mostly picked up in old gardens here'.

Despite her irritating cultural chauvinism, Grahame's book charts her gradual understanding of Tuscan conditions and methods. Reflecting on the finished garden she recalls the wasteland she confronted years before. Though she admits that she would have liked more poppies, larkspurs, delphiniums, lupins and 'suchlike things, in true English fashion', she is pleased with the overall effect. Given the arid soil and scanty water, the absence of equipment and untrained help it is hardly surprising that the local people called her garden a *miracolo*; she, more modestly, describes it as 'a garden of which no one need be ashamed, and one that is never without flowers at any season'.

Towards the end of the book, while describing the olive and cypress dotted landscape beyond her garden walls, Grahame confesses that sometimes in the fresh

ABOVE *Tuberoses. Such floral exuberance would be more in keeping with an Edwardian cottage garden than a Tuscan villa.*

cool air of an Italian summer morning, watching the lights and shadows passing across the fields, she wonders if there was any need to make a garden at all.

Though her attempt to create an English flower garden in the Florentine hills may have been misguided, Grahame's love for the Tuscan landscape finally redeems her insular English arrogance. And perhaps her focus on flowers was not so inappropriate. Though Wharton shocked the horticultural world with her assertion that flowers were but 'a late and infrequent adjunct…a parenthetical grace', the debate still continues as to the place of flowers in Italian horticulture. In the second century B.C. Cato had advocated planting flowers for garlands, a century later Varro advised planting them simply for the pleasure they bring. During the Middle Ages plants were valued chiefly for their medicinal properties, but Europe's conquest of Constantinople in the early thirteenth century introduced tulips, crown imperials, irises, hyacinths, anemones, ranunculi, narcissi and lilies. Boccaccio's fourteenth-century descriptions confirm that flowers feature in the Italian vision of paradise while Botticelli's fifteenth-century paintings attest to the continued love of flowers.

As trade and exploration expanded in the sixteenth century new plants were brought in from the Americas, Africa and the East. Though originally sought for their commercial potential, floral imports soon came to be valued for their novelty alone as the gardens of the elite began to feature special sections devoted to exotic or ornamental specimens. The Medici were among the most avid collectors of rare and beautiful plants, as demonstrated by their Boboli Garden in Florence or the rural gardens of Castello.

Undoubtedly the Renaissance fashion for evergreens, water and sculpture diminished the role of flowers; as Vernon Lee described it, 'when the art of gardening reached its height it took to despising its original material'. Nonetheless in the late sixteenth century, at the height of the Renaissance fashion, Francesco Bocchi extolled a particular Florentine garden, claiming, 'wherever a man turns he enjoys the sweet air, full of the perfume of fruit and of flowers which are ever abundant *according to their season*'. While affirming the affection for flowers, this account reveals the true role of flowers in the Italian garden: they are seasonal features, not permanent fixtures, and their place is outdoors, in the ground, not indoors in vases or pots. Indeed, despite her naivety, priggishness and jingoism, Grahame's floral exuberance may have been closer to the true Italian horticultural style than the austere, evergreen creations of her academic, architecturally-biased compatriots.

While Grahame and her garden have both disappeared, *In A Tuscan Garden* survives as a vivid account of a particular early Anglo-Florentine attitude to the host country and its horticulture. Seven years later Grahame published a second volume, also anonymously, entitled *Under Petraia with Some Saunterings*. An illustrated account of travel in Northern Italy interspersed with musings on Tuscan character and culture, the book reveals as much about the author as it does about the subject. This, and *In A Tuscan Garden* remain a lasting tribute to the mysterious, indomitable, arrogant, exasperating, but ultimately inspiring Georgina Grahame.

BELOW *A long central axis extends from the main entrance, linking the dwelling with the garden and landscape beyond in traditional Renaissance fashion.*

7
A pagan citadel
SIR GEORGE SITWELL'S Montegufoni

SIR GEORGE SITWELL'S DRAMATIC TWELFTH-CENTURY FORTRESS Montegufoni epitomises a strain of foetid romanticism which infused the early Anglo-Florentine community. Imbuing his medieval castle with what Harold Acton described as 'a poetical atmosphere entirely *sui generis*', Sitwell created a series of simple but elegant garden rooms which brilliantly combine medieval and Baroque horticultural features.

Although his *On the Making of Gardens* was published in 1909 and his Tuscan garden was created between the two world wars, Sitwell really belongs to the late nineteenth century, along with Janet Ross seeking Virgilian precedents for her rural life, Vernon Lee exploring Baroque gallants, Lady Paget cultivating her Pre-Raphaelite moonlit meadows and Sir John Temple Leader indulging his medieval fantasies. Such *fin de siècle* escapism took a vaguely morbid turn with the dolorous aristocrat who sought out 'fluteless Pans, headless nymphs and armless Apollos', and found in Italy's old gardens, a pleasing air of 'neglect, desolation and solitude'.

Although he designed an Italianate garden for his gothic family seat in Derbyshire, Sitwell created a gothic garden for his Tuscan estate. Having spent several decades exploring the Italian peninsula while researching his book, Sitwell purchased the Castello di Montegufoni in 1910. Originally a settlement rather than a single architectural unit, the castle began as four houses within a fortified wall. The first official records of the estate date from 1135, and it is thought that the title Lord of Montegufoni was created by the Margrave Matilda in an effort to retain the region's loyalty in the ancient disputes between emperor and pope.

By the thirteenth century the castle belonged to the Acciaiuoli family, who, like the Medici and Caponi, were prominent Florentine bankers. In 1386 the central tower was constructed, reminiscent of the Palazzo Vecchio with its assertion of power and grace. It was not until the sixteenth century that the original houses, now seven in number, were joined into a single unit. In the seventeenth century the chapel was built and the eastern and northern façades were added, contributing a Baroque façade to the medieval fortress. It was also at this time that the formal gardens were laid out with the steep drop transformed into a balustraded forecourt above two grass terraces, accessed by a double ramp enclosing a grotto.

A sundial attached to the northeast wall is inscribed 1699, the year of the villa's zenith. From this point Montegufoni appears to have slowly sunk into decrepitude, until it was purchased by Sir George on the anticipated proceeds from his recently published magnum opus. The castle, chapel, some surrounding farmhouses and twenty-two acres cost him 120,000 lire, a purchase which Sitwell justified to his son Osbert claiming: 'apart from the romantic interest, [it] is a good one as it returns five per cent. The roof is in splendid order, and the drains can't be wrong, as there aren't any.' The letter also mentions the remains of a terraced garden, a grotto and some statues.

One of Sitwell's first acts as the Lord of Montegufoni was to purchase musical instruments for the local villagers. Forming a band, known affectionately as the 'Philharmonic Society of Montegufoni', they would serenade guests on summer evenings and provide the music for Sitwell's grand balls. While he eschewed any physical participation, Sitwell welcomed the rustic charms of the agricultural season. Even his cynical son Osbert, constrained by noble birth or effete constitution, delighted in the spectacle in which his only role was observer:

> We like the short hot days in September [when] the figs and grapes are carried inside the castle inside enormous oval-shaped baskets. During this period the peasants move slowly through the vines picking the grapes and the air is redolent with the smell of the must that seeps out of the vats while the great purple stains on the stone floor show where the grape juice has been spilled.

In 1925 Sir George Sitwell moved permanently to Italy to avoid England's punitive post-war taxes. It was only then that he turned his attention to the garden proper, having spent the intervening years rehousing the 300 peasants who inhabited the castle and removing the architectural accretions as well as the various grain and vegetable plots which had accumulated round the grounds. Although he relied on architecture rather than plants for his effects, Sitwell filled the surrounding slopes with Tuscan roses which, 'like all else in good taste', were unobtrusive, forming pointillist masses of colour that did not distract from the view.

Restoring the central courtyard to its medieval austerity, he removed a large oleander, replanting it in the Cardinal's Garden to the west. Indeed, Sitwell was something of an expert at repositioning trees; Osbert recalls how, as a child returning, periodically, from boarding school, he could gauge his father's mood by the position of two trees in the front lawn which were raised and lowered according to Sir George's whim.

To emphasise the medieval mood of the courtyard, Sitwell installed pyramids of stone cannonballs which provided the only ornamentation beyond an ancient wellhead and a few potted plants. He then set about restoring the western terrace. Guarded by a pair of worn stone lions, this precipitous space was protected from the cliff edge by a line of cypresses on one side and a wisteria-covered pergola on the other. In the centre of this small formal space he planted the oleander, which was then surrounded with gravel paths and scrollwork parterres. Although today the parterres overflow with colourful geraniums, in Sitwell's day they contained sober stocks and plumbago, a concession to his wife's pleas for colour and scent. Now known as the English Garden after its creator, Sitwell called this area the Cardinal's Garden after Nicola Acciaioli an earlier inhabitant who was made a cardinal in the early eighteenth century. Each afternoon Sitwell would establish himself in the Cardinal's Garden, perched in an uncomfortable wicker deckchair, presiding, like some latter-day Pan, amid the perfume of rose and wisteria.

BELOW *Sitwell's elaborate tufa-lined grotto, with its glittering mosaic floor, mirror encrusted walls, frescoed ceiling and elegant sculptures, is a far cry from the natural caves which inspired the earliest garden grottos.*

ABOVE *With its enviable position overlooking the main Florence/Volterra road, and near the important Via Francigena by which pilgrims from northern Europe travelled to Rome, the early lords of Montegufoni made their fortune by levying duties and tolls.*

In the early 1920s, while Sitwell was preoccupied with the gardens, his sons, Osbert and Sacheverell, commissioned the Italian Futurist Gino Severini to fresco one of the grand halls within. Brilliantly combining cubist forms and traditional *commedia dell'arte* figures, the artist created a charming, if slightly camp, evocation of the *otium* of villa life. Drawing the surrounding countryside into the dark interior, Severini created a delightful scene of languid harlequins and melancholy musicians – inspired perhaps by the Montegufoni Philharmonic Orchestra – cavorting against a background of rolling hills, stately cypresses, spreading olives and dusty aloes. Though initially sceptical of the project, Sitwell was delighted with the result and immediately commandeered the space, known as the Hall of the Masks, for his own private salon.

In 1931 Sitwell extended the formal grounds and recreated the terraces below the castle ramparts. Cloaking the bastion walls in roses, he laid out the upper terrace as a lemon garden, its long grass avenue lined with citrus trees, many in their original seventeenth-century pots. The lower terrace was left to wild flowers and fruit trees with an iris walk along its outer edge creating an informal link between the formal gardens above and the daisy-filled vineyards below.

With blithe, if not determined, indifference to the political conflagration brewing around him, Sitwell completed the gardens in 1939 with the restoration of the eighteenth-century grotto. Having been occupied for several centuries by peasant families, the grotto was restored with a central sculpture of a loosely-clad woman surrounded by angry peasants and bewildered frogs. Evoking Ovid's tale of Latona,

LEFT *It took Sitwell years to re-house the many tenants living in the castle grounds; when he finally turned his attentions to the garden he discovered several families were still squatting in the grotto.*

it recalls how, bullied by peasants while fetching water for her babies, Latona appealed to her lover Jupiter, who turned her persecutors to frogs. A painted ceiling depicts Jupiter in godlike majesty, while peasant figures surround the walls – one etiolated stone-throwing youth looking remarkably like the young Sacheverell. While Louis XIV's famous Latona fountain at Versailles warned courtiers of the perils of gossip, Sitwell, whose precocious offspring were notorious publicity-seekers, probably appreciated the plasticity of the scene rather than any allegorical significance.

Sadly Sitwell had little time to enjoy his newly restored grotto; with the onset of the Second World War he retreated to Switzerland and died soon after, leaving the castle to his eldest son Osbert. In 1942 when Florence was threatened with bombardment, the city's artworks were stored for safety in surrounding villas. Despite being owned by the enemy, Montegufoni presented an ideal cache with its large halls and discreet position. One of the grand halls was renamed the 'Office of Monuments and Fine Arts'; in this guise it housed 261 works by such artists as Botticelli, Uccello, Cimabue, Giotto and Raphael. Although the castle was commandeered first by the German SS as a residence, then by the Allies as a look-out, the only damage to the artworks was a knife-wound to a Ghirlandaio tondo, reputedly used by German officers as a dining table.

While fighting reached the fields around the estate, the castle itself was largely unscathed though it harboured several hundred refugees from the surrounding villages. During this time the gardens probably reverted to a medieval squalor of anxious livestock, scratching chickens and fiercely guarded patches of vegetables.

After the war Osbert used Montegufoni as a second home while retaining Renishaw, in England, as his primary residence. Through lack of money and lack of interest, he left the place virtually unchanged, though his essays and poems reveal that he was not immune to its charms. His 1954 *The Four Continents*, provides a surprising paean to Tuscany's ancient towers, in which he confesses that Montegufoni, 'stands at the very centre of this country of towers, and from time to time I climb up the steep stairs of my own tower there, in the morning or at night, to allow the feeling of the country round to permeate my consciousness'.

As in the pre-war days Osbert and his sister, the alarming poet Edith Sitwell, filled the castle with illustrious guests, such as composer Constant Lambert, conductor William Walton and artist John Piper. In 1965 Osbert moved permanently to Montegufoni, partly, as his father had done, to avoid British taxes, and partly because he preferred the climate.

Sir Osbert died in 1969 and was buried at the Protestant cemetery of Allori nearby. Three years later his heir and nephew, Sir Reresby Sitwell, sold the castle to a local family, the Posarellis. Unable to maintain the estate on the proceeds of farming the Posarellis turned it into holiday accommodation. A swimming pool was discreetly inserted into the lower terrace and today the castle thrives on Tuscany's buoyant tourist trade.

Despite sharing its horticultural passions, Sir George Sitwell is curiously absent from the memoirs of the Anglo-Florentine community. Although Harold Nicholson and Vita Sackville-West visited while staying with Sybil Cutting in 1923, Cutting's daughter, Iris Origo, makes no reference to Sitwell in any of her autobiographical writings. Already old and curmudgeonly when he settled in Italy, Sitwell had little time for the hyper-intellectual community. He began writing *On the Making of Gardens* after suffering a nervous breakdown, which he delicately described as 'a period of broken health...the effects of over-work'. While his essay attests to the beneficial effects of horticulture, it remains more a therapeutic exercise than a practical text. In its own time it was virtually ignored; today its appeal remains the author's enchanting prose, loquacious style and passion for his subject. A threnody to Italy's neglected gardens, it captures the particular attitude of a small and rather recherché community at a unique moment in history.

RIGHT *Osbert Sitwell, heir to Montegufoni. Like his siblings Edith and Sacheverell, Osbert, the 5th Baronet, was an aesthete, a patron and a notorious snob. He is remembered for his five-volume autobiography which is full of tales of his exasperating father, though he did concede that Sir George's knowledge of Italian gardens was 'unrivalled'.*

8
A garden of delights
PRINCESS GHIKA'S Villa Gamberaia

ABOVE *Widely considered the most exquisite of all Tuscan gardens, Harold Acton praised Gamberaia's 'serenity, dignity and blithe repose'.*

OPPOSITE *A perfect foil to the elegant gardens which surround it, the austere villa is distinctly Tuscan with its deep projecting eaves, heavily coigned edges and erratically placed windows.*

ALTHOUGH IT IS NEITHER PARTICULARLY GRAND NOR HISTORICALLY IMPORTANT, the Villa Gamberaia is perhaps the best loved of all the Anglo-Florentine villas. Since it was purchased, in 1896, by the reclusive Romanian Princess Ghika it has provided inspiration to generations of garden makers and has called forth encomia from nearly every visitor. Geoffrey Jellicoe pronounced it more Italian than the Italians themselves; Charles Latham described it as a place of 'perfect loveliness'; Rose Nichols enthused 'time has only mellowed its beauty and no discordant innovations have been allowed to mar its harmonious ensemble'; Harold Acton declared it the most poetical of the Florentine gardens; Bernard Berenson called it 'one of the *fari* [beacons], one of the haunts of my life'; Iris Origo simply proclaimed it the most beautiful, and the most romantic, garden of them all.

Dramatically set in a wooded hillside, with distant views of the Duomo beyond, Gamberaia combines, in a modest three and a half acre site, all the features of classic Italian horticulture. Edith Wharton was one of many who marvelled at its variety and compactness, describing it as 'the most perfect example of the art of producing a great effect on a small scale'. This effect begins with a long cypress-lined approach which leads to an austere Palladian villa, set on a flat plateau. Spreading out from the villa are a grotto, bowling green, nymphaeum, bosco, *limonaia* and a modern water garden, all encircled by a balustraded stone wall embellished with urns and statuary. The Baroque lemon garden has four parterres surrounding a central pool. Below it is the grotto, accessed by a wrought-iron gate embellished with Florentine lilies. Although this area is often called a secret garden because of its high enclosing walls and delightful *giochi d'aqua* (water games), Acton charmingly describes it as an 'open-air boudoir'.

The most famous feature of the estate however is the water parterre which fills the eastern plateau. Originally an orchard, in the eighteenth century the space was transformed into an elegant scrollwork parterre ending in a *garenna* – an artificial island where rabbits were kept. A hundred and fifty years later the parterre had degenerated into a scrubby kitchen garden, which the princess, with the help of her gardener Martino Porcinai – father of the modernist landscape designer Pietro Porcinai (1910–86) – transformed into a dazzling horizontal hall of mirrors with four rectangular sheets of water animated by simple fountain jets. In the princess' time these were embellished with a pink Edwardian froth of water lilies, rose trellises, oleander bushes and cascading geraniums; today an austere monochrome prevails with topiary hemispheres and obelisks rising from the surrounding hedge. The circular shape of the ancient *garenna* is retained in a semicircular pool, while the space is enclosed at the eastern end with an arcaded exedra of clipped cypresses framing views of the city below.

Despite the dramatic serenity of the water garden, many Anglo-Florentines gushed even more lyrically over the bowling green. This thick band of emerald turf legitimised the English love of lawns, disproving the theory that grass had no place in Italian horticulture. A 250 yard long terrace at the back of the villa, it creates a longitudinal axis extending the length of the property from the dense woodland nymphaeum in the west to the open hillside in the east. This runs parallel to a shorter longitudinal axis, running from the entrance gate, along the approach avenue, through the villa, to bisect the water garden and end in the views of Florence framed by the exedra hedge.

A transverse axis, about half the length of the bowling green, cuts through the villa from the rustic grotto at the back to the formal terrace in front, linking the agricultural hillside above, to the village of Settignano below. This simple cruciform layout imposes order on the various elements. Indeed, throughout the garden space is carefully manipulated as wide, open plazas vie with dense, dark enclosures, magnificent panoramas contrast with tightly framed views and clipped greenery echoes carved stone to integrate natural and man-made into a single harmonious whole.

In a community which charted its own activities in forensic detail, remarkably little is said about the inhabitants of Gamberaia. The princess, Catherine Jeanne Keshko Ghika, a Romanian by birth, was sister to Queen Natalie of Serbia and married to the Albanian Prince Eugene Ghika. A famous beauty in her youth, she is said to have shut herself in seclusion when she began to lose her looks. As a child, Iris Origo was told the princess would emerge at dawn to bathe in the pools of the water garden and at night she would pace the long cypress avenue, but all Origo ever saw of the mysterious creature was a glimpse of a veiled figure at an upper

BELOW *The long grass axis connects the various elements of the garden, linking the closed grotto to the north with the open views to the south, the enclosed garden to the east with the lawn to the west, the dense, vertical woodlands behind the villa with the open horizontal terraces in front.*

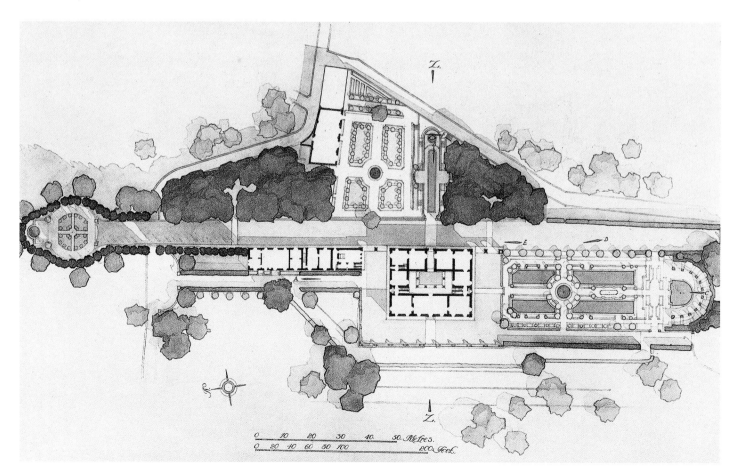

ABOVE *With its harmonising of solid and liquid, stone and water, image and reflection, the water parterre is a brilliant modern interpretation of the Baroque style.*

window. Bernard Berenson, a near neighbour, less romantically described Ghika as a narcissistic Romanian lady whose only interests were herself and her garden – a view substantiated by her own niece who, according to Charles Quest-Ritson, described the princess as hating 'both men and mankind'.

Ghika's companion, Miss Florence Blood, is described variously as British and American. She was clearly less reclusive than her soulmate as she appears in Mary Berenson's diary as an occasional visitor. Nicky Mariano, having befriended Blood's niece at school in Florence, was invited to several Sunday afternoon receptions at the villa. Although no mention is made of the princess, Mariano describes Miss Blood as gracious and welcoming, a small, dainty woman in a long velvet dress with a magnificent blue-grey Angora cat.

It is rather fitting that these two mysterious ladies should inhabit a villa which began, in the fifteenth century, as a convent of Benedictine nuns. The name Gamberaia, meaning 'the place of the crayfish', possibly derives from a nearby pond where locals caught the eponymous *gamberi*, although it is more likely that it was bestowed by the Gambarelli family which owned the property in the sixteenth century. In the early seventeenth century Andrea di Zanobi Lapi acquired the property and in 1610 he commissioned the present villa, as indicated in an inscription on the architrave: *Zenobius Lapius erexit ac fundavit AD MDCX*. Lapi inhabited the property for 60 years, obtaining permission from his neighbours to conduct water

through their properties to supply the estate. In 1636 a local widow accused him of stealing her water – apparently the dispute is still unsettled – but Lapi eventually acquired enough water to create the garden which remains, largely in tact, today. Zocchi's 1744 engraving shows the cypresses in the entrance drive still separate and only waist high; by 1901 Janet Ross, in *Florentine Villas*, was describing the cypresses as towering 'like dark green steeples'. Today they are clipped into a dense green wall flanking the entrance avenue.

After Lapi died the property passed to his nephew, Giovanni di Lapi, who bankrupted himself expanding the garden. In 1717 Gamberaia came into the Capponi family – whose villa south of the city has a similarly long, lush bowling green, as prescribed by Alberti to provide a space for games. Giovan Vincenzio Capponi (1693–1748) was a botanist and founding member of Florence's Botanical Academy; it was probably during his stewardship that the garden acquired its current layout. The Capponis sold the villa in 1854 and it changed hands frequently over the next decades, for many years being let out as summer lodgings – a dubious fate to which Wharton attributes the almost complete preservation of its Baroque design and planting.

With its mysterious owners, spectacular setting and magical gardens, the Villa Gamberaia was a source of fascination to the Anglo-Florentines. Le Blond informs her readers that it is not possible under any circumstances to see the villa while the owner is in residence, but assures them that when the owner is absent, permission may be sought from the princess' agent in Florence. Clearly many took advantage of these absences.

In 1924 the property was bought by an American woman, Matilda Cass Ledyard, Baroness von Ketteler. It was she who simplified the water parterre, replacing the exuberant flowers and shrubs with a more austere, modernist palette of evergreen box and yew. Von Ketteler abandoned the property in 1938; during the Second World War it was used for storage by the German army and both villa and garden were badly destroyed when a retreating officer set fire to the villa.

In early spring 1948 Bernard Berenson visited from his own Villa I Tatti nearby; his diary entry, published in *Sunset and Twilight*, reveals the reverence which many in the community felt for Gamberaia. Having found the villa burnt out, the statues and vases broken, the grounds neglected with broken trees and unmown grass, he still avers:

and yet the place retains its charm, its power to inspire longing and dreams, sweet dreams. Its beauty, though so uncared for, is still great enough to absorb one almost completely, the terraces, the ponds, the great apse of cut cypresses, the bowling green as you look at it from the grotto toward the south like a great boat sailing through space, the view over the quiet landscape of the Chianti hills and further over domes and towers to the snow-capped Apennines and the Arno glimmering in the plain.

In the 1950s the baroness gave the estate to the Holy See and soon after it was bought by Marcello Marchi, who rebuilt the villa and restored the grounds. His descendants still run the estate, opening the garden and renting parts of the villa for receptions and conferences. Despite this new public incarnation, the Villa Gamberaia retains its intimacy, elegance and variety; it is generally considered the most perfect small garden in Tuscany.

BELOW *A path from the villa's back door leads to the grotto garden – a sensuous, mysterious space whose high mosaic embellished walls and exuberant sculptures once hid secret water games.*

9
Arcadia recovered
VERNON LEE'S Il Palmerino

ABOVE *This is one of several portraits of Lee painted by John Singer Sargent, whose dedication 'to my friend Violet' is scratched in the top right hand corner. Like Lee, Sargent was the offspring of peripatetic expatriates. He was born in Florence where he and Lee played as children and remained lifelong friends.*

OPPOSITE *The elegant villino where Vernon Lee spent her final decades. Here her greatest pleasure was 'conversation with friends' till deafness isolated her, fuelling a reputation for aloofness.*

ALTHOUGH TODAY SHE IS VIRTUALLY UNKNOWN, Vernon Lee (1856–1935) was among the most formidable, and the most formative, of the Anglo-Florentine community. Her villa, Il Palmerino, is a small, square, stuccoed building, hidden by high stone walls, backing onto unkempt fields, off a steep road at the edge of the northern hill village of San Domenico.

While her garden was hardly noteworthy, Lee herself was one of the most influential shapers of Anglo-Florentine horticultural tastes. A waspish bluestocking, she was born Violet Paget, but adopted the gender-neutral pseudonym to ensure her work would not be dismissed as mere 'women's writing'. E.M.Forster might well have been thinking of her when, in *A Room with a View,* he described the elusive expatriates:

> Living in delicate seclusion, some in furnished flats, others in Renaissance villas on Fiesole's slope, they read, wrote, studied, and exchanged ideas, thus attaining to that intimate knowledge, or rather perception, of Florence which is denied to all who carry in their pockets the coupons of Cook.

Henry James described Vernon Lee as 'the most able mind in Florence', before warning that she was 'dangerous and uncanny as she is intelligent, which is saying a great deal'. Maurice Baring called her, 'by far the cleverest person I have ever met in my life and the person possessed of the greatest range of the rarest culture', while Bernard Shaw praised her as, 'the noblest Briton of them all'. Within the community Bernard Berenson valued her, Janet Ross resented her and Iris Origo was daunted by her. Nicky Mariano, Berenson's assistant, observed: 'her face, in spite of its snout-like ugliness, was fascinatingly witty and intelligent'. Even Cyril Connolly gave her the dubious distinction of bracketing her with Coleridge, Swinburne, Wilde and Melville as 'mighty-mouthed international geysers'.

Born in Germany in 1856, to an eccentric English mother and a timid French father – who first entered the household as her older half-brother's tutor – Vernon Lee belongs as much to the nineteenth as to the twentieth century. Although most of her writing was done while Queen Victoria was still on the throne, she was, at heart, a modernist with a precocious interest in psychology. An outspoken pacifist, feminist and anti-vivisectionist, she adopted the international uniform of the cultured lesbian, with man's shirt, knotted scarf, velvet jacket and long skirt. Fiercely intellectual, prodigiously well educated and extraordinarily versatile, she produced travel pieces, poetry, fiction, biography, short stories and plays on subjects ranging through history, politics, religion, philosophy, ethics, music and aesthetics.

Although known as much for her trenchant views and spiky personality as for her extraordinary literary output, Lee is best remembered for her essays; typically these were elegant ruminations which describe a subject in sensuous detail, drawing in an astonishing range of literary, artistic and historic allusions. While fluent in English, French, German and Italian, publishing in each of these languages, Lee's first love was Italy and her writing shaped the English view of post-Renaissance Italy. Her knowledge of the country was legendary, her villa was an international gathering place, and the presence of this famous intellectual inspired independent women of means to settle in the vicinity.

Where an earlier generation had been attracted to Italy by the romance of its republican struggles, Lee was inspired by its more distant past. To a nation that had spent decades locked in the struggle for independence, Lee helped recover a sense of former grandeur, writing essays on such diverse subjects as eighteenth-century academies, the old Bologna road and Tiberius' villa. Nor could she resist the allure of that perennial favourite, 'Bonnie Prince Charlie', writing a biography of the Countess of Albany, the wife of the dissolute Young Pretender. But Lee's greatest facility was her ability to convey the *genius loci*, the spirit of a place, and her chosen place was Tuscany, the love of which imbues her writing.

Like many late nineteenth-century Anglo-Florentines, Lee was enchanted with Italy's pagan origins, describing the country as 'a land where the past haunted on, with its wizards, sphinxes, strange, weird, curious'. This flirtation is perhaps a reflection of a post-Darwinian atheism, a search for the divine in a world where God had been displaced but neither Freud nor Marx had come along to fill the void. As Maurice Baring claimed, 'she had worshipped the Lares and Penates of ancient Italy all her life, and knew the rituals and respect that should be paid to them as well as to the Christian saints who had taken their place'. Long before Sir George Sitwell wrote his paean to decaying Renaissance gardens, Lee was divining pagan goddesses in Italy's old villas.

After a pattern of winters in Germany and summers in France, Lee's parents discovered the Italian peninsula when the Franco-Prussian war of 1870–71 made sojourns in France unwise. They settled permanently in Florence in 1879 to provide a stable home for Lee's half-brother, an aspiring writer whose nebulous illness coincided with the publication of his precocious half-sister's first teenage essays. Settling with the family at 5 via Garibaldi, Lee wrote her books between nursing her brother, enduring her own neurasthenia, fulfilling her filial duties, entertaining guests and retreating from Florence's inferno-like summers to canvass publishers in England.

In 1889, seeking fresh air, a garden and respite from visitors, Lee convinced her family to leave the city. In the village of San Domenico, just below Fiesole, they

ABOVE *The villa was built in the early fifteenth century by Ottaviano Antonio di Duccio, thought to have been a jeweller to the Medicis. In 1855 it became a monastery for the friars of Santa Croce; it was later sold to an Italian count who rented, then sold it, to Vernon Lee.*

found Il Palmerino, a square yellow farmhouse nestled among the hedged fields and dusty unpaved lanes which Tuscans still call 'white roads'. Taking a seventeen year lease on the property, the Pagets proceeded to furnish the house with antiques, carpets, books, paintings and the usual accoutrements of expatriate life. Despite such embellishments, however, it retained a rustic charm especially in comparison with such distinguished villas as Janet Ross' noble Poggio Gherardo and Bernard Berenson's elegant I Tatti nearby.

Il Palmerino was essentially an urban villa, its front façade abutted the public road, with only a small lawn to the side and the farm buildings directly behind. Though Wharton described the garden as 'homely', the grounds were large enough for Lee's father to hide in during social engagements; one bemused visitor recorded her surprise on learning that the man she had encountered several times in the garden was, in fact, her host's husband.

In Lee's time the lawn was a small formal garden with gravel paths between four box parterres around a central fountain. Today an iron and glass greenhouse at the far edge, probably dating from the late nineteenth century, has a staircase rising to its roof to create a raised belvedere for viewing the countryside and Florence beyond. The stable block, covered in wisteria, is linked to the villa with a stone terrace which was often deployed as an outdoor theatre where Lee would perform her own works. An illustration in the villa archives suggests that at some point a gallery ran along the wall which linked the main house to the stable, creating a raised stage area. The stables themselves were later developed into an elegant dwelling with a gravel terrace in front, giving onto a small, formal garden which overlooks the surrounding farmland. Paths meander through the abandoned fields, though remnants of stone terracing attests to earlier cultivation. The major feature of the grounds, a huge umbrella pine by the gate, was lost in the severe storm of 1985.

Despite several detailed property maps drawn in Lee's own meticulous hand, the villa's archive has no garden plans, though the many paths suggest that her preference was for natural walks rather than formal gardens. Certainly the preponderance of bluebells, cosmos, nasturtiums, zinnias, marigolds and anemones now running wild, reveal a love of simple cottage plants.

Within the timeless setting of her suburban villa Lee entertained friends and visiting luminaries, first as the unmarried daughter of the house, then after her parents' deaths, as the hostess in her own right. One Italian guest recorded summer evenings dining al fresco, beneath the vine pergola 'with the table lit by candles in glass globes and the fire flies dancing on the corn behind the little garden'. Although the pergola has long gone, an ancient *fragola* grape by the stables recalls those enchanted evenings.

Dining al fresco is one activity the Anglo-Florentines appear to have reintroduced to the Italian garden. Boccaccio's fourteenth-century protagonists frequently direct their stewards to bring the supper outdoors, and the Villa Lante's famous outdoor stone dining table indicates that Renaissance cardinals copied the example of the ancients; by the nineteenth

BELOW *Il Palmerino embodies the handsome yet severe dignity of Tuscan domestic architecture which, as Henry James suggested, seems designed more to keep people out than to invite them in.*

century, however, the practice appears to have fallen from fashion. Janet Ross, Lee's arch rival, also created a vine-covered bower for outdoor dining; Iris Origo recounts how she had to entice her Italian husband to dine on the terrace on summer evenings when the wheat fields were alight with fireflies and the air perfumed with nicotiana. In *The Last Edwardians* John Phillips recalls visiting Violet Trefusis in Villa L'Ombrellino, where, on fine days, they would lunch on the front terrace amid the gardenias and azaleas or on the more intimate side terrace, guarded by eighteenth-century stone blackamoors: 'Violet always picked a gardenia, a boutonnière for each gentleman present…'.

Vernon Lee was left as the sole proprietor of Il Palmerino in 1896 when her mother died and her brother underwent a miraculous recovery and disappeared to America. The following year a furore ensued when Bernard Berenson accused Lee of plagiarism, suggesting that an article on aesthetics she had written with her companion, Kit Anstruther-Thomson, was a distillation of 'numerous conversations I have been privileged to have with you at the Palmerino, and of even more numerous visits with Miss Anstruther-Thomson to the galleries'. Berenson frequently accused old friends of plagiarism, and given Lee's exhaustive studies in the subject the accusation seems unlikely, nonetheless the resulting rift split the Anglo-Florentine community for decades.

ABOVE *Lola Costa,* Giardino*, c.1934. In her time Vernon Lee was known for her trenchant essays and pioneering work on aesthetics. Today she is being rediscovered as an early role model for independent, intellectual women, a rediscovery prompted by the English-born painter, Lola Costa, who purchased the villa on Lee's death.*

In the early 1900s, after separating from Anstruther-Thomson, Lee rented some buildings behind her villa to a widowed acquaintance, Irene Forbes-Mosse, immortalised as 'Ira' in Elizabeth von Arnim's 1898 *Elizabeth and Her German Garden*. When the estate came up for sale in 1906 Lee purchased it outright, raising funds by selling Forbes-Mosse a thirty year lease to convert some of the buildings into a *villino* or small house.

Despite the modesty of her garden, whose simplicity might well have been determined by her frail stature and lack of wealth, Lee was widely hailed as an expert on Italian horticulture. Wharton dedicated *Italian Villas and their Gardens* to 'Vernon Lee, who, better than any one else, has understood and interpreted the garden-magic of Italy'. Indeed it is unlikely that the book could have been written without Lee, who acted as mentor and guide, introducing Wharton to villas near Florence, and providing introductions to a range of villa owners stretching from the northern lakes to the Roman campagna.

While the exact nature of their relationship is unclear, Wharton was clearly enchanted on her first acquaintance with Lee, whom she described as a 'highly cultivated and brilliant woman'. Though only six years her senior, Lee provided a rare model to the fledgling young writer: successful, independent, powerful and professional, she was one of the few women writers with whom Wharton forged a deep friendship. One of Wharton's travelling companions, Percy Lubbock – who would later marry the prominent Anglo-Florentine Sybil Cutting – provides a vivid picture of the two women in garden-visiting mode with Edith briskly checking out every detail while Lee, ruminating beside her, slowly evolved an image of the past, animating the space with her brilliant speculations as to its previous inhabitants, activities and appearance. In later life a *froideur* arose between the two women, provoked, perhaps by Wharton's growing intimacy with the Berensons, nonetheless Lee's influence on Wharton was profound.

Despite her reputation as an expert, Lee published very little on the subject of Italian horticulture, and has thus been rendered a mere footnote in garden history. Her major contribution, however, is her rediscovery of the Baroque at a time when the style was widely dismissed as vulgar and decadent. In an essay entitled 'Old Italian Gardens', published in *Limbo* (1897), she charts the shift from the simple flowery orchards and meads of the fifteenth-century humanists to the architectural gardens of the sixteenth and seventeenth-century Renaissance princes. Acknowledging the influence of *Hypnerotomachia Poliphili*, she observes, 'Here we find trees and hedges treated as stone and brick work; walls, niches, colonnades, cut out of ilex and laurel; statues, vases, peacocks clipped in box and yew.' She also celebrates the Baroque style, noting its sympathy with the antique and pointing out that its sinewy exuberance mimics nature, harmonising the man-made with the natural to create an ideal style for garden statuary and design:

> The antiques do well in their niches of box and laurel under their canopy of hanging ilex boughs; they are in their weather-stained mutilated condition, another sort of natural material fit for the artist's use; but the old sculpture being thus in a way assimilated through the operation of earth, wind and rain, into tree trunks and mossy boulders, a new sculpture arises undertaking to make of marble something which will continue the impression of trees and waters, wave its jagged outlines like the branches, twist its supple limbs like the fountains.

While conceding that it might be 'mistaken as indoor decoration', Lee asserts that the Baroque has provided 'the only works which are thoroughly right in the open air', its rhythmic curves echoing the undulating landscape and its bold ornamentation complementing the exuberance of nature.

In 1883, during her annual summer migration to London, Lee attempted to place a series of articles on the 'Outdoor Renaissance'. Had she been successful her place in horticultural posterity might well have been assured. Nonetheless references to Italian gardens permeate her essays and her first book was inspired by her discovery, at the age of fifteen, of Rome's charming baroque Bosco Parrasio. Located on the Janiculum, the city's highest hill, the Bosco was created for the Arcadian Academy, a fashionable arts club whose members assumed shepherds' names, adopted the pan pipes as their emblem and promoted the pastoral form in drama, poetry and music. Banned in 1699 from their quarters in the Orti Farnesiani the Arcadians commissioned a new meeting place with an elegant casino and a sylvan amphitheatre, surrounded by woodland embellished with fountains and sculptures.

With its integration of baroque ornament and romantic setting this garden was a crucial influence on the precocious teenager. Her essay on the Arcadians, published in 1878 in *Fraser's Magazine*, became the core of her first book, *Studies of the Eighteenth Century in Italy*. In the introduction Lee describes the Bosco, stressing its picturesque decrepitude: 'muddy paths, dripping bushes, flower-beds filled with decaying ilex-leaves, lichen-covered benches, crumbling plaster and mouldering portraits – grim spectres looking down on the final ruin of Arcadia'. Delighted by the morning glories smothering the amphitheatre, she discovers the casino inhabited by market gardeners who hang their hats on the poets' busts and store their tools in the mouldering gaze of 'sad, haggard poetesses in sea green…draperies'.

Towards the end of her working life, in an essay written just before the First World War, Lee once again discovers an 'inexpressibly romantic' place, turreted and battlemented, with a vast jade-green fish tank and portico bearing the traces of ancient fresco work. Of the seventeenth-century judge who transformed his farmhouse into this delicate, scholarly place, Lee observes: 'one got the idea of a self-respecting and scrupulous man of law, a fine scholar withal, living retired among friends, very modestly, but with a certain research and finish in all he did, visible…in the clipped hedges, the elaborate sundials, even in the scalloping of a mere corner of wall enclosing the garden'. The Anglo-Florentine intelligentsia for whom she was writing would have seen echoes of the author herself in this modest but diligent scholar who transforms a mundane farmhouse into an elegant villa.

While Lee's taste for the Baroque was taken up by the succeeding generation of Anglo-Florentines, most of these were fiercely competitive males who failed to acknowledge her influence. Though Berenson promoted early Renaissance artists, he developed his villa and garden in a distinctively baroque fashion; while Sir George Sitwell relished the romance of his twelfth-century castle, he created a baroque garden surround for the lower levels of the estate. Despite its medieval origins Arthur Acton restored his villa to its baroque rather than any earlier incarnation. More importantly however, Lee's love of the Baroque infused the young architect Geoffrey Scott, whose 1914 *The Architecture of Humanism* remained a seminal text for several generations.

In 1914 the pacifist Lee left her villa in the care of her Italian staff and retreated to London. 'In Time of War', one of her final essays, sounds the death knell for her favourite subject: 'among the many things, spiritual even more than material, which the war will have wrecked…is the cult of the genius of places'. After regretting the destruction of various French, Italian and, controversially, German towns, she laments even more the spiritual vandalising of those places which have been 'sacked, burnt, defiled ten thousand times over by millions of indignant wills and by imaginations thirsty for reprisals'. Shocked at the animosity between Europe's greatest nations, appalled at the vengefulness directed towards the country of her birth, she spent the war years railing against the destruction of Germany.

In 1920 Lee returned to Il Palmerino. Finding the villa too large, after a protracted legal battle she took over her tenant's *villino*, renting the main house to recompense Forbes-Mosse for her earlier expenses. In 1922 Mary Berenson brokered a rapprochement with Berenson, noting tersely in her diary, 'Miss Paget came to lunch and she and BB outdid themselves in glittering lies of a general nature'. Too deaf to hear Berenson's low, soft voice, Lee carried a large ear horn, but raised it while she herself was talking and dropped it the moment she was expected to listen. Nonetheless, as two ageing, vulnerable foreigners in a diminishing community, they rediscovered their common love of art.

In the 1920s, having been introduced to the joys of driving by Edith Wharton, Lee traded her pony cart for a small car in which her factotum would transport her round the countryside. One of her final essays describes her perennial longing to see the hills beyond Siena, adding, 'now, at last, thanks to the modern miracle of motor cars, I have been among those hills'. In her little *villino*, with her newly purchased motor car and a smattering of guests to amuse her, Vernon Lee lived out her days in the care of three ancient servants. Kinta Beevor, who visited as a child, claims that despite the cropped hair and stiff collars, Lee was particularly kind to children and was renowned for the enchanting presents she gave. When she died in 1935 Lee's ashes were deposited in the English Cemetery and her library was donated to the British Institute, where visitors can still peruse the most fashionable books of the time with Lee's pithy comments jotted in the margins.

Il Palmerino was purchased by an English-born painter, Lola Costa, and her Italian husband Federigo Angeli. During her first year at the villa Costa painted an image of the *villino* showing a gravel terrace giving onto two symmetrical box parterres around two lilac trees. A central avenue is flanked with potted lemons, and a double iron arch at the end frames a rural landscape punctuated with the ubiquitous cypresses and pines. It is unclear whether this garden was designed by Forbes-Mosse before the war, or by Lee herself when she took over the *villino*, nonetheless this is the garden in which Vernon Lee spent the final decades of her life. Despite its simplicity and modesty, lacking both statuary and water, the design suggests the harmonious blend of Italian formality and English embellishment which characterises the best Anglo-Florentine gardens.

Inspired, perhaps, by their shared English ancestry Costa worked to preserve Lee's memory, and her grandchildren are now developing the villa as a guest house, hoping the reputation of its illustrious forebear will entice visitors to savour the views which sustained Vernon Lee throughout her adult life.

BELOW *A plaque on the villa commemorating Vernon Lee records: 'From her youth she loved Italy and spent her long life and rare intellect in the perfecting of that understanding and in the passionate search for beauty. Her books remain to prove it.'*

10
A rural sanctuary
JOSEPH LUCAS' villa in San Domenico

ABOVE *In Lucas' much loved Mural Fountain water slides from the mouth of a marble mascaron into an oval dish before dropping into a larger stone trough. Extolling its 'liquid music' Lucas placed a reading bench nearby to benefit from the 'lulling monotony' of its 'rhythmic song'.*

OPPOSITE *Domenico Ghirlandaio,* The Dormition of the Virgin, *c.1490 (Tornabuoni Chapel, Santa Maria Novella, Florence). The Fiesole hillside often features in the background of Renaissance paintings; Lucas delighted in this historic setting, frequently referring to the venerable Villa Medici which towered above his own less illustrious but equally ancient villa.*

ALTHOUGH VIRTUALLY NOTHING IS KNOWN ABOUT HIM, Joseph Lucas, in his 1913 *Our Villa in Italy,* recorded the joys of Anglo-Florentine villa life so vividly that the book went into a second edition almost immediately. From the very beginning his flowery prose reveals an almost irrational passion for Florence: 'the City of the Lily cast its spell over us, and we are still fettered in the toils of its witchery and wish to remain so even unto the end'. Being neither scholar, socialite nor dedicated horticulturist, Lucas does not feature in any of the many biographies of the time, and unlike most of the community he only lived in Florence for part of the year, returning home to England every summer because, he asserted, an English country house, surrounded by an English garden is 'the best place out of Paradise during the summer months'.

Seeking to escape the English winters, Lucas and his wife set out to find an ancient Tuscan villa with a large garden, full of trees casting deep shadows 'with here and there a sombre cypress, lofty and distinguished, watching like sentinels over the welfare of the household'. His initial wish list was both precise and extensive, including magnolias, camellias, oleanders, lemon trees, mimosa, a south-facing loggia to catch the winter sun, a *podere* in which to grow peaches, pears, figs, plums, apricots and cherries, plus a vineyard and an olive grove to provide him with wine and oil.

While Arcadia permeated the Anglo-Florentine imagination, so too did the Medici, and after discounting various properties as too gloomy, too expensive or too far from Florence, Lucas was finally seduced by an unnamed villa in San Domenico, largely because of the imprimatur of the Medici who had colonised the area 500 years before. Lucas frequently evokes Lorenzo and his brilliant circle in the Villa Medici above, Cosimo worshipping at the San Girolamo convent nearby, and Giovanni presiding in the Badia abbey just over the hills before he was made Pope Leo X and obliged to decamp to Rome. Fra Angelico, the fifteenth-century painter who lived in the local monastery, and Boccaccio, whose *Decameron* is set in the surrounding countryside, are also frequently cited, as is the beauty of the Italian spring, which is described as a Botticelli painting, with wild flowers creating 'a garden of gods and a playground of fairies'.

Bewitched by the setting, intrigued by the historical, artistic and literary associations, Lucas agreed to pay 10,000 lire for the fourteenth-century villa. Although it came with a sitting tenant with a three year lease to run, Lucas found the view, the crumbling terraces, ancient lemon house and, in particular, the potential to create a garden, worth the price and the wait.

The villa itself stood simple and square with a loggia projecting at the southwest corner. While soothing green jalousies and deep overhanging eves kept the interior cool through the summers, there was little respite from the bitter winter weather. Retreating from the wind which whistled through the outer rooms, Lucas colonised the central hall; here he and his wife received friends, drank tea, read, wrote and played bridge, warmed by a large American stove. On warm spring days they would throw open the French windows of the gloomy dining room and take their meals under the fir tree in the garden.

Stability, security, age and order were the hallmarks of the villa; Lucas frequently extols its traditional craftsmanship, lichen-stained walls and simple, harmonious façade, constantly comparing his ancient dwelling with the shoddy architecture of the present. Indeed the book is, in many ways, a rant against the modern world. Like many Anglo-Florentines, Lucas carefully researched the history of his estate. Built on the site of an old stone quarry, its earliest known owners were apparently the Buoniusegni from whom a local dyer had bought it in 1475. Lucas points out that his villa was located far enough from the urban upheavals that, 'the rage of the mob could break itself to pieces before it climbed the hill...even if vengeance was burning in its heart'. The class antagonism which he so vividly evokes probably had a contemporary resonance in the agitation which was stirring the working classes in Italy and England at the time.

When buying the villa, Lucas had to purchase the surrounding ten acres separately from the tenant farmer who had used the space as a market garden. After leasing the bulk of the land to a professional farmer, Lucas himself retained a few acres to plant an olive orchard and a small vineyard. This soon yielded him a hundred barrels of wine and six barrels of oil – a barrel being the equivalent of fifty litres or eleven gallons.

Unable to find a gardener to help him on the grounds, Lucas convinced Enrico, the tenant farmer, to take on the job. A forty year old bachelor, Enrico lived in a house in the olive grove with his mother, her niece and a blind brother. Having worked the estate for over 250 years, the family was no longer able to survive; even when reduced to market gardening they could not compete with cheap imports. Although struck

LEFT *Lucas claimed an Italian garden without a fountain would be 'like a piano without music in it, like poetry without rhythm' and duly constructed a fountain pond.*

RIGHT *Lucas removed a decrepit two hundred year old* limonaia *to create the loggia and rose clad pergola. The cross beams were made from the* limonaia's *roof timbers while the lichen-stained, weather-toned roof tiles were redeployed on the gardener's cottage.*

by Enrico's dignity and wisdom, Lucas could not help noting his primitive working methods, recording that in Tuscany they still comb the soil with a hand plough, sow seed and trust to Providence and a fine climate to furnish the crop.

Once his vineyards and orchards were established, Lucas turned to the garden. The sloping site was already divided into two terraces connected by a flight of stone steps. These were flanked by pillars, topped with noble creatures – lions, dogs or griffons whose features were worn to indecipherability. Visitors stepped directly from the reception room on to the gravel terrace, beyond which was a grass lawn which Lucas enlivened with small flower beds. Beneath the fir tree in the corner he placed the inevitable wicker chairs and dining table, while several yards away a decorative stone wellhead protected the precious water supply.

The lower terrace, having long been used as a lumber store, was in poor shape when Lucas arrived, but it was here that he created his small, formal Italian garden. As Enrico repaired garden paths and reset the stone borders, Lucas restored the iron entrance gates, erecting an arch to support the roses which had climbed up the piers to smother the crowning eagles. He then designed a large, central, marble basin with a single jet – inspired, no doubt, by Boccaccio's fountain in the *Decameron*.

With the framework repaired, Lucas turned to the planting, inheriting with the villa over 70 potted lemon trees, 200 small and 100 large pot plants. He then proceeded to stuff the steps, banks and parterres with roses and spring bulbs: ranunculus, anemone, narcissus, tulip and iris. He also incorporated flowering shrubs such as the crimson blossomed *Cydonia cardinalis* and the golden rosetted *Kerria japonica*. Finally he created a ribbon of low green hedges around the flower borders and beds with 1,500 cuttings Enrico had nurtured from two ancient box trees in the *podere* – a sobering reminder that before the ubiquitous garden centre every plant had to be begged, imported from specialist nurseries or grown from scratch.

Like Georgina Grahame before him, Lucas was surprised to discover that in Tuscany flowers were cultivated as a cash crop. When he finally convinced Enrico to

grow flowers for their own sake, Lucas proudly reported that he was able to provide the local English church with 'basketfuls, basketfuls of flowers – daffodils, carnations, roses, lilies', weekly from January to May. A lean-to glasshouse, heated by flues, also enabled him to produce early lilies-of-the-valley, calla lilies, white lilac, freesias and twice-weekly plates of asparagus in January and February. Next to this was a more substantial *limonaia,* for over-wintering the potted citrus, without which no respectable Italian garden could exist.

While Medici moguls delighted in breeding exotic – and erotic-shaped – fruits, the Anglo-Florentines were more attracted by the link between lemons and Greek mythology; lemons were said to be the golden fruit that Hercules stole from the garden of the Hesperides and brought back to Italy. With such symbolic value to add to their sensuous delights, it is hardly surprising that most expatriates aspired to a few potted lemons if not an actual lemon garden. Pots were known by the number of men it took to move them; four, six, eight and ten-man pots were not uncommon, though Lucas proudly describes his two prized hundred year old trees as residing in rare 'fourteen-men pots'.

The lemons themselves were the source of some tension in the household as Lucas' cook often sold the surplus lemons in the market and then forgot to credit him with the receipts. Lucas also recounts how a friend with many lemon trees could not understand why lemons routinely figured in the housekeeping expenses until he met the cook one morning en route to the market with several lemons poking from her bag; he realised then that she would take them from his trees, then bring them back as though she had bought them. Lucas wryly notes that as oranges have no market value they never tempted a cook to deceit.

Once the formal lines of his garden were established, Lucas added a lilac border to the east to hide the farm buildings of the *podere*; beside this he placed a long grass walk – a feature which may well have been inspired by the bowling green of the near by Villa Gamberaia.

Although Lucas set out to create an authentic Italian garden, his final work, with its colourful shrubs, abundant roses and floral exuberance, owes as much to English as to Florentine tastes. In this, as in much else, Lucas encapsulates the Anglo-Florentine experience, taking refuge from the modern world by cultivating a garden abroad. The consolation he finds in Tuscany's ancient countryside, antique architecture and archaic traditions suggests a man in retreat from a world which was, at the time, marching towards a catastrophic conflagration. Even allowing for Edwardian hyperbole in those dying days of empire, his book is an extended eulogy for lost sureties. Frustratingly it gives no indication of his own identity and the second edition gives no account of the later history of the villa.

Today, in the village of San Domenico, nestled below the Villa Medici, down a narrow road beside the monastery – just as Lucas describes it in 1913 – there is a villa surrounded by vineyards and orchards with a small enclosed garden on two terraces, which resembles the blurred photographs in Lucas' book. Perhaps, unlike its owner, his unnamed villa did survive the terrible turmoil of the twentieth century.

BELOW *The main street of San Domenico. Though tiny, San Domenico was a cosmopolitan gathering place. Lucas records that the local tram contained 'all nations, kindreds and tongues – English, American, German, French, dusty Orientals and sometimes Italians'. Even today the village fountain carries a plaque inscribed with the names of Italians and foreigners who were inspired by the local countryside.*

11

Last refuge of the aesthete
THE ACTONS' La Pietra

ABOVE *Describing himself as the last aesthete, Harold Acton embodied the leisurely, cosmopolitan world of the Anglo-Florentines. His autobiography exhorts: '(We) are neither famous nor spectacular. But…it is our duty to remind our fellow creatures of what they are fast forgetting, that true culture is universal.'*

OPPOSITE *A dramatic 800-metre cypress avenue frames the villa. Cypresses figured prominently in the Anglo-Florentine imagination, winding up the hillsides, punctuating the landscape, shielding distinguished villas from the outside world.*

RISING REGALLY FROM THE OLIVE TERRACES, approached by a long cypress-lined drive, La Pietra is the grandest and most illustrious of the Anglo-Florentine estates. For two generations its owners, the Actons, presided over the expatriate community, amassing an enviable art collection, restoring their splendid villa and hosting the city's most eminent visitors. Though long associated with the aesthete and scholar, Harold Acton (1904–94), La Pietra was, in fact, the creation of his father.

Arthur Acton (1873–1953) arrived in Florence in the 1890s to work as an artist, having studied first at the Beaux Arts School in Paris. Though his son avers that Acton painted 'intermittently', he soon evolved a lucrative sideline as agent to the American architect Stanford White. As America's pre-eminent classical architect and interior designer White had an insatiable need for Renaissance artefacts – artefacts which Acton supplied, with scant regard for their authenticity. Mabel Luhan said of Acton, 'He looked as though he were made of wax, and the faint, pretty smile on his small, kind mouth seemed to proclaim him as utterly harmless; but later, when I knew him better, he revealed an interesting, hard, and quite impervious nature.'

In 1903 Acton married an American heiress, Hortense Mitchell, whose brother, Guy owned the villa Il Guillarino, next to the Villa Capponi south of the city. As Hortense was the daughter of a fabulously wealthy Chicago banker, the couple moved into La Pietra, a magnificent fifteenth-century villa one mile north of the city on the old Bologna road.

Named for the milestone at its gate, La Pietra had a suitably illustrious history. Harold Acton traces the story back to the Middle Ages when the estate belonged to the Macinghi family, eight of whom, he proudly recounts, served as priors of the Republic. In 1460 the villa was sold to the Sassettis, who handled the French banking interests of Cosimo de' Medici and later Lorenzo the Magnificent, and who, 'according to an ancient chronicle', descended from early Saxon kings. Encompassing both the fledgling republicanism of the priors and the royalty of the Saxons, the Middle Ages as well as the Renaissance, La Pietra's pedigree was unrivalled within the Anglo-Florentine community.

Under the Sassettis the estate evolved from *villa rustica* – a rural estate supplying produce for the family's urban needs – to *villa urbana* – an elegant country dwelling devoted to leisure and study. Reflecting the peace and prosperity of the times the castellated farmhouse was expanded to create a Renaissance palace. It was probably at this time the *limonaia* was added to the end of the walled orchard on the north side. It was probably also at this time that the grille-work was added to the rusticated ground floor windows; such features were popular among the newly rich to evoke the defensive dwellings of the turbulent Middle Ages and imply a long and noble ancestry.

A fifteenth-century plan of the villa depicts a *giardino grande* at the back, a *giardino segreto* to the south and a central courtyard with a well.

In 1546 the Sassettis sold the property to another prominent banking family the Capponis. Over the next three centuries they renovated the estate, and in the early seventeenth century they embellished the rear façade of the villa with their coat of arms, though the Sassetti arms were retained, below, to demonstrate the building's noble heritage. In 1608 the Capponi arms were surmounted by a cardinal's hat when Luigi Capponi achieved that ecclesiastical position. Harold Acton attributes the renovations to Carlo Fontana (1634–1714), who had trained under Bernini and worked mostly in Rome. As the cardinal would probably have begun the remodelling soon after attaining office and Fontana was not even born until nearly two decades later, this attribution is rather fanciful, but, like his compatriots, Acton, keen to link his villa to illustrious figures, was unlikely to enquire too deeply into the legends surrounding its past.

Whoever oversaw the villa's remodelling, the cardinal demanded that the central portion of the house be raised to accommodate a ballroom appropriate to his new status. Similarly he transformed the exterior, covering the walls with golden stucco, adding elegant pediments and framing the massive windows in the local grey stone. Capponi also added the two handsome gatehouses and decorated the walled garden. Typical seventeenth-century *rocaille* scrollwork of shells and pebbles ornament the walls which were then crowned with alternating urns and busts. Harold suggests that it was at this time that the central courtyard was covered over and the elliptical staircase was introduced, adding that when his father restored the villa in the early twentieth century he placed a marble fountain – 'attributed to Benedetto da Maiano' – on the space where the well would have been. Although attributing this particular feature to the cardinal gives it greater romance, the roofing of the courtyard is as likely to have happened in the nineteenth century when many Florentine villas had their loggias glassed in and their internal courtyards covered for the comfort of expatriate inhabitants who rented or purchased the villas from their original Italian owners.

Although little is known of the villa's eighteenth-century incarnation, a fresco on the ground floor near the present kitchen depicts the estate with two walled gardens flanking the main house, and a causeway linking it, across the valley, to the main road. In the nineteenth century the Capponis sold the villa to a Prussian family; in the mid-nineteenth century it was inherited by the Incontri family and whatever gardens existed to the south and rear were swept away to create the *giardino inglese* with a shrub-dotted lawn sweeping up to the villa.

In 1907, having rented La Pietra for several years, the Actons purchased the 57 acre estate including the villa and four other dwellings. Arthur Acton immediately began what his son later dubbed 'the process of tuscanization', replacing the nineteenth-century parkland with formal gardens. Ultimately eight and a half acres would be devoted to gardens with much of the rest of the land given over to olive terraces. Harold described the olive groves in quasi-religious terms: 'the olives pruned like chalices, were centuries old, increasing in fertility with age, and they filled the valley with a silvery smoke…'. In fact, olive trees throughout the region were pruned in a cup shape to ensure the greatest possible exposure to the sun.

Though the Actons took no part in the actual farming of the land, Harold reveals a characteristically Anglo-Florentine enchantment with the seasonal activities of the local *contadini*. Describing the ever popular grape harvest, in which his only role was as spectator, he celebrates the autumn as the season of glamour 'when grapes

ABOVE *Arthur and Hortense Acton in the outfits designed by Poiret for a Persian soirée at the Villa Palmieri just before the First World War. Costume balls and amateur dramatics were favourite entertainments in those antebellum days.*

festooned the whole expanse, dropping to the cracked earth in heavy purple clusters and figs of many kinds oozed beads of ripeness.' He goes on to describe the white oxen which waited patiently to bear away the harvest, concluding, 'For the contadini this was the climax of the year, and they gave vent to their joy in songs that were sunshine vocable, hymns to the sun.'

Elsewhere he recalls the annual agony of having to return to school in the vintage season, when Florence was at her most delectable. And again: 'To enter Tuscany in September is to enter Arcadia. The countryside is dedicated to the vine, and the city is half asleep, the palaces empty.'

Though Arthur Acton is generally credited with the garden's design, various professionals have been associated with the project. Georgina Masson attributed the layout to 'the late Arthur Acton and his Polish gardener'. Recent scholarship, however, has questioned Acton's role. Penelope Hobhouse mentions the French garden designer Henri Duchêne (father of the more famous Achille), while Harold makes no reference to any designer, claiming only that his father restored the garden on pure Tuscan lines and with all the ingenuity of a sixteenth-century architect.

It is unlikely that such a grand architectural enterprise could have been overseen by an amateur like Acton; furthermore, a stone inscription in an isolated corner of the garden acknowledges the leading figures behind the restoration as Mariano Ambroziewicz, Pasquale Bonaiuti, Giuseppe Castellucci, H.O. Watson and Edwin Dodge, one-time husband of Mabel Dodge Luhan who provides such insights into Acton's character. In the brochure they give out to visitors, the trust which currently owns the estate rather defensively notes that Arthur made initial drawings and plaster topographical models, adding that it is unlikely that he would have relinquished final authority in the project. While the ultimate authorship may never be determined, clearly Arthur Acton was the guiding spirit behind the garden's design.

Curiously, both the commemorative plaque and Harold Acton's memoirs refer to the project as a 'restoration'. Given that there was little, if anything, left to restore, the work would more accurately be described as a recreation, revival, homage or, indeed, a pastiche. This misleading claim of authenticity by the Actons *père et fils* demonstrates, yet again, the Anglo-Florentine obsession with linking themselves to the past.

RIGHT *The garden theatre in the 1930s when Florence attracted a glittering company of 'reprobates and literati'. Here live performers – amateur and professional – vie with sculptured figures to animate the green stage.*

RIGHT *William Merritt Chase,* An Italian Garden, *c.1909 (Chrysler Museum of Art, Norfolk, Virginia). This impressionistic oil painting depicts La Pietra's walled orchard, known as the* pomario. *In summer, when the lemon trees were set out in their baroque pots, the lemon house at the end was often deployed for impromptu dining and concerts.*

ABOVE *The villa rises over the gardens, framed by the crowns of umbrella pines which echo curves of the topiary spheres and fountain.*

Acton's first horticultural act at La Pietra was to remove the false acacia trees flanking the 850 yard causeway. Inspired, perhaps by the Boboli's dramatic cypress alley, he lined the approach with cypress trees. For the young Harold, cypresses emblemised Tuscan villa life. Exiled at school in England, he filled his exercise books with sketches of these noble trees, and when the term was finally over and he was once again travelling south, the first glimpse of cypress 'quivering with dark yet intimate mystery in the Ligurian sunshine, filled me with an ecstasy like the kiss of the beloved after an age of separation'. But where Boboli's avenue was lined with classical statuary and grassed to create a gentle walk, Acton's trees grew into a dramatic, dark green tunnel, whose severity he relieved with an inner row of *Rosa chinensis*, locally known as May roses or *la rosa d'ogni mese*, 'the monthly rose', as they flower from March to November.

As the only remnant of the baroque garden, the orchard was one of the first areas Acton restored, repairing the *rocaille* work, dividing the space into eight box-edged beds for vegetables and planting the enclosing walls with espaliered fruit trees. He then embellished the utilitarian space, smothering the walls with banksian roses, planting iris and violas along the base of the walls, growing flowers in the vegetable beds and flanking the gravel paths with potted citrus trees, over a hundred of which were over-wintered in the elegant baroque *limonaia* at the end of the garden. Harold later recalled the narcotic potency of the enclosed garden:

the juciest peaches clustered by the *rocaille* walls, haunted by emerald lizards, and the Californian tomatoes hung heavily, softening and reddening in the sun….In the warm water of the central fountain frogs forgot to leap into hiding under the flat lily leaves and stared upwards as if hypnotised while thirsty dragonflies flashed past for a quick sip and bloated goldfish mouthed at insects drunk with honeysuckle.

Following the classical tradition, the formal gardens at La Pietra were conceived as a series of outdoor rooms, linking the villa to the surrounding countryside with terraces, parterres, hedged walks and dramatic framed vistas. Florence is visible, obliquely, in the valley ahead and Fiesole, equally obliquely, on the hilltop behind.

The main gardens, created from the steep slope at the back of the villa, were laid out in a series of broad terraces. The top terrace abutting the villa is a long gravel platform, enclosed by a stone balustrade, adorned with statues. Flanking staircases lead to the terrace below, known as the *prima vasca* because of the oval basin at its heart. This, and the *seconda vasca* below it, contain grass lawns, gravel paths and box-lined parterres, all enclosed by low walls and clipped hedges. The lowest terrace is bounded by a colonnade separating the formal garden from vineyards beyond. At the centre of this, dramatically sited against a background of cypresses, stands a statue of Hercules, his strident masculinity rather undermined by the lush wisteria dripping around him.

Paths from the central terraces lead to hedge-enclosed rooms containing dozens of pieces of stonework and statuary including exedras, portals, pergolas, balustrades, vases and busts. One axis leads to a *tempietto,* or temple, centrally placed in an open lawn. Another ends in a heavy Colossus by Orazio Marinali, a seventeenth-century sculptor who provided statues for Andrea Palladio's villas on the Veneto.

In a totally different mood, the green *teatrino* at the end of another axis has boxwood footlights and 'wings' peopled by Francesco Bonazza's graceful, eighteenth-century genre figures. As the famous green theatre at Villa Garzoni near Lucca survived the First World War unscathed, it may well have provided the inspiration for this whimsical feature. The archives at La Pietra are full of photographs of cavorting figures, suggesting that through the 1930s the theatre was the focus of the outdoor entertainments.

In true Italian fashion, La Pietra is essentially a green garden. Sunlight and shadow are as important as plants and statuary. Verticality is provided by tall, enclosing hedges whose severity is relieved by clipped topiary drums and the occasional topiary peacock. Colour is incidental, but the range of cypress, boxwood, laurel, holm oak, umbrella pine, grass and lavender ensure a variety of shade and tone.

To the Anglo-Florentine community, La Pietra's garden appeared as authentic as the villa it surrounded; indeed Harold Acton proudly boasted that most visitors thought it a product of the sixteenth rather than the twentieth century. Today its anachronisms are more evident; the golden Irish yews conflict with the Tuscan greens of the garden. The overlay of Dorothy Perkins and banksia roses, tumbling geraniums and dripping wisteria set the garden firmly in the Edwardian tradition, though it remains a fascinating example of the early twentieth-century interpretation of the classical style.

One significant element to the understanding of La Pietra – judiciously over-looked by both Harold Acton and the trust which now owns it – is that Arthur Acton must have designed the garden, at least in part, to display his statuary to potential

BELOW *The grounds at La Pietra displayed Arthur Acton's collection of statuary which included balustrades, benches, exedras, fountains, mascarons, pavilions, pools, portals, sculptures and urns. The twin cypresses at the end created a focal point that reinforced the central axis.*

customers. Although his propitious marriage allowed him to eschew the vulgar role of common dealer, it appears that everything in La Pietra was negotiable; as Mabel Luhan reported: 'They say, my dear, you can buy anything in his villa if you want it.'

Despite the discretion with which the Anglo-Florentines carried out their commerce, dealing was common in the community. In her 1878 *Friendship*, Ouida's unscrupulous protagonist purveys newly-minted antiquities to naive visitors, embellishing her villa with the wares she wishes to sell. Although this was, reputedly, a portrait of Janet Ross, it could equally describe Arthur Acton. Two generations later, in his 1925 *roman-à-clef*, *Those Barren Leaves*, Aldous Huxley's lugubrious Mr Cardon claims of the Anglo-Florentine penchant for dealing, 'It has the charm of being more dishonest than almost any other form of licensed brigandage.' He expatiates on how dealers take advantage of the ignorance or poverty of the vendor to get the work for nothing, then exploit the snobbery and equally profound ignorance of the buyer to extort from him a fantastic price.

> What huge elation one must feel when one has succeeded in bringing off some splendid coup! Bought a blackened panel from some decayed gentleman in need of a new suit, cleaned it up and sold it again to a rich snob who thinks that a collection and the reputation of being a patron of the ancient arts will hive him a leg up in society.

Though Arthur Acton was a pillar, if not a foundation stone, of the community, he was known, in his own time, as a scoundrel. Berenson, in private correspondence, described him as 'a bounder', adding, 'but he has a flair for good things'. Some believe Acton retreated to Florence after clashing with the British police for photographing under-aged girls, others believe it was the Italian police with whom he clashed. In any case such vices were not uncommon. Kinta Beevor records that Colonel George Keppel kept a studio for 'artistic poses'; adding: 'everybody adored his wife, Alice Keppel, King Edward VII's favourite, and he must have felt left out'.

In that era of Charles Dodgson and Julia Cameron, when photographs of naked children freely passed as art, Berenson's assessment of Acton might stem, instead, from his putative relationship with the young Italian aristocrat, Ersilia Beacci, by whom he is said to have sired a daughter. Indeed, Harold avers that 'nearly all the old Florentine families had Anglo Saxon ramifications', although he refused to acknowledge any Italian ramification in his own.

Through the 1930s, the Actons, like many Anglo-Florentines, ignored the rising tide of Fascism. Writing later about life in the 1930s, the expatriates were quick to distance themselves from the regime. Despite rigged elections and suppression of the press most had little exposure to Fascist atrocities, believing that the traditional enmities between families and villages were simply being expressed in the allegiance to different parties; the red flag of the Socialist and the black flag of the Fascist being

ABOVE *During the Second World War La Pietra hosted recuperating officers. Harold Acton wrote of that time, 'It is hard to connect war with so tranquil a site, and I like to think that some of our men were able to rest here between the endless slogging of that obstinate, bitter campaign. The benign spirit of the place must have refreshed them. One young English lieutenant would sit out in the garden all day, as in a dream, before he went over the Futa to meet his death.'*

but a modern iteration of the battle between Guelphs and Ghibellines. Returning at the end of the 1930s after a decade away, Harold Acton expected talk of war but found the only subject on people's lips was the king and Mrs Simpson.

Despite their widespread acceptance of Mussolini, however, under *Il Duce* there was a subtle change in attitude towards the expatriates. Servants turned sullen, no longer considering themselves part of the family. Ironically, the mantle of the ancients, promoted by the Anglo-Florentines, was given a sinister new interpretation by young Italians revelling in their unexpected victory in Abyssinia/Ethiopia. Suddenly the nation believed itself to be the heir of ancient Rome with all her imperialist ambitions.

As often happens in times of turmoil, the expatriates simply turned away and quietly cultivated their gardens. Acton recalls: 'As foreigners we kept aloof. My father continued to improve the garden and his collection of paintings, undisturbed.' The Second World War, however, destroyed the Actons' idyll. Hortense, whose American citizenship made her an enemy alien, retreated to Switzerland, while Arthur waited too long and had to bribe his way out of the country to follow her. The Fascists then confiscated Acton's art collection, and though it was later returned, he never recovered his faith in the country or its people. When his younger son died during the war, Arthur turned the estate over to Harold. After his father's death in 1953 Harold shared La Pietra with his mother until her death in 1962.

A celebrated poet at Oxford, Harold is reputed to be the inspiration behind the decadent aesthete Anthony Blanche in Evelyn Waugh's *Brideshead Revisited*, not least because, like Blanche, he recited T.S.Eliot's *The Waste Land* from a megaphone at a Worcester College garden party. When it became clear that he would not reach the literary heights of his early promise, Harold abandoned fiction. Distressed at the spread of Fascism, he left Florence in 1932 and settled eventually in Peking. There he explored opium, Buddhism and oriental mores until the threat of war in 1939 forced him back to Europe.

While it is tempting to attribute La Pietra's camp exuberance to the younger Acton, Harold had nothing to do with the design or furnishing of the villa. Describing himself as 'the last aesthete', he spent his life preserving the legacy of the Anglo-Florentines. Under his stewardship, La Pietra's gardens softened as trees grew unchecked, topiary went uncut and self-seeded flowers proliferated. More interested in history than horticulture, Harold's homage to his patrimony was his 1973 *Tuscan Villas,* a comprehensive survey of local estates with accompanying photographs by his long-term companion, the Austrian photographer Alexander Zielcke.

Following the Anglo-Florentine tradition, Harold also wrote books on such Italian subjects as *The Last Medici* (1932) and *The Last Bourbons of Naples* (1961). This pre-occupation with decline is also evident in *Tuscan Villas*, which ends with the impassioned plea that the villas be rescued from the neglect to which many had already succumbed.

On his death in 1994 Harold bequeathed the estate with its five villas to New York University, to be used for academic purposes. The five grandchildren of his father's putative mistress, Ersilia Beacci, are currently claiming the share of Arthur Acton's estate – valued at between 100 and 500 million dollars – that would be their due in law if his paternity could be proved. Meanwhile New York University is engaged in a massive 15 million dollar restoration project, and every summer the garden hosts a range of elegant entertainments, from concerts and readings to dramas and balls, recreating some of the glamour of the garden at the height of its Anglo-Florentine incarnation.

BELOW *Harold Eberlein's 1922 plan of la Pietra reveals the geometry of the villa's layout with its central axis extending from the top terrace to the pergola overlooking the vineyards below. Peripheral paths running parallel to the slope lead to garden rooms enclosed in hedges and statuary. The theatre had not yet been built below the orange garden and the cistern had yet to be transformed into an elegant grotto.*

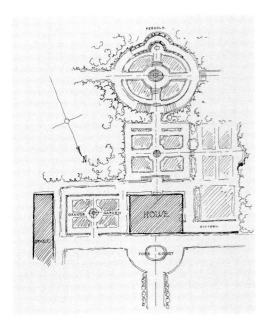

12
Majesty and carelessness
MABEL LUHAN'S Villa Curonia

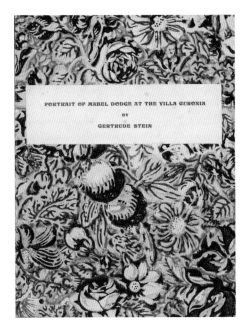

ABOVE Portrait of Mabel Dodge at the Villa Curonia *is a verse portrait by the alarmingly avant-garde Gertrude Stein, a frequent visitor to the villa before her companion Alice Toklas brought the friendship to an abrupt end.*

OPPOSITE *Sharing the Anglo-Florentine penchant for dressing up, Luhan quickly adopted the Renaissance attire appropriate to her ancient villa.*

THE MUCH-MARRIED AMERICAN HEIRESS MABEL DODGE LUHAN followed the Anglo-Florentines' template in fleeing social strictures at home to settle in an ancient dwelling, create a garden and indulge in the fantasy of Renaissance life. While her villa quickly receded from view after its brief moment of fame, Luhan's account of Anglo-Florentine life, recorded in her 1935 *European Experiences,* is amusingly irreverent. Neither a scholar nor an artist, Luhan was an astute observer; as one of the few members of the community who moved on, she is sharper in her observations than most of its chroniclers.

Born in 1879, the only child of a very rich family of bankers in Buffalo, New York, Luhan married at twenty but was widowed two years later when her husband was killed in a hunting accident, leaving her with one child. In 1904 she remarried the Boston architect Edwin Dodge who joined her in search of a life of beauty and art. After testing France they bought into the Anglo-Florentine ideal, arriving in the city in 1905.

For many months they scoured the hills around Florence with a succession of unsatisfactory agents. Clearly a difficult woman to please, Luhan admits, with disarming candour, that she wanted a villa filled with space, light, grandeur; but also a place of 'poetic and tender charms' in which she could be 'both majestic and careless, spontaneous and picturesque, and yet always framed and supported by a secure and beautiful authenticity of background'. Her demand for light was particularly difficult since most Florentine villas were built facing north or east to keep them cool and shaded in the summer.

After rejecting most of the available properties – including the famous Villa Medici, Fiesole, which she felt was too public and overlooked – Luhan finally found the Villa Curonia in Arcetri, a village just south of the city where Milton and Galileo are reputed to have met. Like many Anglo-Florentines, when unable to trace a memorable predecessor Luhan aggrandised her villa by association with illustrious neighbours. Describing her new dwelling as 'not very far from the Villa Pazzi', she suggests, with no supporting evidence at all, that her villa might have been built by the grand dukes who took over that infamous dwelling where the assassination of Lorenzo the Great and his unfortunate brother had been planned half a millennium before.

The villa itself was reached by a steep road winding from an entrance gate guarded by a small lodge where the gardener Pietro and his sinister wife, the black-browed Rosita resided. Like many Anglo-Florentines, Luhan had an ambivalent relationship with the *contadini* on whom she depended. While she adored the blue-eyed Pietro, she believed that his wife belonged to a secret society with members all over Italy who stole things from their masters and sent them away to sell. Such paranoia was not

unusual within the community; Luhan's close friend and neighbour Lady Paget condemned all *contadini* as 'short-sighted and childish', Georgina Grahame described them as suspicious, inept and conceited, while Iris Origo, more ecumenically, damned them as 'illiterate, stubborn, suspicious and rooted, like countrymen all the world over, in their own ways'.

Luhan's villa, perched like a crown on a flat, buttressed plateau, presided over a steep hill of terraced olive groves. Florence glimmered below, the Apennines rose to the north, the plains of Pisa swept out to the west, to the east a cluster of cypresses blocked out the neighbours and to the south Rome beckoned beyond the waves of low hills. The villa itself was a long, low dwelling, two rooms deep. A wide double door topped by a fanlight opened onto the cold northern garden, while the roofline of the southern terrace arched up in a great false curve to contain a painted clock surrounded by elaborate scrollwork.

Inspired by the rumour that Raphael had once lived in the villa, Luhan had her husband remove bits of plaster to see if his frescoes lingered beneath. Though no Raphaels were found, Luhan's disappointment was assuaged by the discovery of an interior courtyard. Noticing a crack in a storeroom wall one afternoon, Edwin began chipping away at the plaster and soon revealed a large stone column topped by a perfect Corinthian capital. What eventually emerged was a perfect fourteenth-century *cortile*, two storeys high with vaulted ceilings. Describing it as her 'Brunelleschi court', Luhan furnished the space with faded silk banners discarded from some ancient horse race, whose turquoise, vermilion and yellow embroidery shimmered against the grey stone walls.

As Luhan furnished the interior, her husband, who had studied architecture at the Beaux Arts school in Paris, turned his hand to the exterior. While he removed generations of architectural accretions to restore the villa to its Renaissance splendour, she created new accretions, demanding a music room to run the length of the western end of the villa with a loggia opening onto the formal garden below. She also added a square bay window extending from her bedroom over the southern terrace, lined with window seats and enclosed with coloured glass leaded windows. The attentive Pietro planted jasmine to twine up from the terrace and surround the window to perfume his mistress' sleep.

Luhan's southern terrace was a sunny, intimate space scented with a large daphne and a yellow rose which climbed up the wall to frame the second storey windows. To maximise the sun on this side of the villa Edwin cut the windows down to the ground and turned them into glass doors. Meanwhile Luhan erected an iron pergola linking the garden door to an ilex bower beyond. Draping the pergola in yellow, white and pink 'Dorothy Perkins' roses, she created 'an outdoor flowery boudoir' furnished with tiny tables and green chaises longues. Finally, terracotta tubs of gardenias were arranged along the edge of the terrace to bathe the area in scent.

Hidden in the lawn beyond, a well, unusually sunk level with the ground, was boarded up when one of Luhan's dogs drowned in its depths. At the end of the lawn Luhan also discovered a secret garden, the far wall of which was frescoed with a faded scene of a fisherman standing by a lake.

Whatever misgivings the Anglo-Florentine garden makers had about Tuscan nurserymen, clearly they were expert arborists with sophisticated techniques for growing, transporting and transplanting trees. When Edwin determined to create a cypress-lined approach he purchased cypresses, 'as large as would bear transplanting'. Luhan immediately softened with an inner planting of May roses 'the small, pink single rose that blooms nearly all the year round'. She later added a thick band of iris to create a line of blue along the base of the dark green cypresses – an effect which was probably inspired by Ross' approach at Poggio Gherardo. At a bend halfway up the drive, framed in a semicircle of cypresses, she placed a colossal statue of Atlas struggling beneath his globe – a feature which suggests the influence of Arthur Acton, on whose gardens Edwin Dodge had consulted.

As with many of her cohort Luhan was more interested in people than places; she admits: 'I believe I only really *knew* Italy in the early days before I made friends there'. Unfortunately, although her autobiography is filled with gossip and intrigue she was never particularly interested in the anglophone community, or perhaps she was simply never accepted by them, especially after she ostentatiously embraced the disgraced Marchese Bindo Peruzzi di Medici, whom the whole of Florentine society had cut because of a homosexual scandal revealed by his spurned mistress.

On their arrival in Florence, the first Anglo-Florentines Luhan got to know were the Actons; indeed, she cattily describes Arthur Acton as a dealer with a shop which his wife made him hide. He also inspired her observation that for many in the community objects were as important as people. It is hardly surprising therefore, that Harold Acton makes no reference to her Villa Curonia in his *Tuscan Villas*, although he does mention her briefly in *Memoirs of an Aesthete*: 'she had come from Buffalo to absorb Florentine impressions, which begot a herd of Buffalo memoirs a couple of decades later'.

After Luhan had completed the restorations to her villa and garden, her dear friend, neighbour and social advisor, Lady Paget 'commanded' that she have an 'at home'. The strict organisation and the hierarchy of invitees reveal that Anglo-Florentine bohemia was quite as rigid as any other society. Indeed Luhan notes that despite the affection between them, she always felt that Paget found her vaguely outlandish:

'she took to one in spite of one's race, and she would even try to help me overcome it, or make the best of it'. Despite their friendship, Paget fails to mention the young American in any of her memoirs; she does however confirm Dodge's suspicions about her snobbery, noting in her diaries:

> What I detest about Florentine society is that all the men and some of the women are of such uncertain *nationale*. One does not know where they come from, or where they got to. Many of them are rather amusing, but one never feels sure of what they may or may not do.

Under Paget's watchful eye Luhan planned her social debut – a late afternoon reception over which she presided in a Renaissance robe. The glass doors of the salon were opened onto the terrace; the ancient damask and velvet hangings were enhanced with music, soft light and roses; the dining table was laid with 'a Medician feast' of flowers, fruit and luxurious foods: mounds of *dolci*, pitchers full of wine, champagne and coffee, all followed by chocolate and cigarettes. The delighted hostess pronounced the whole effect 'Tintorretish'.

Everybody came, Italian aristocrats and English expatriates, strolling about the garden, discreetly examining the decor, remarking on the music: 'a beautiful voice arose singing the Evening Star song from Tannhauser, and there was a murmur of delight…for such songs were still able to awaken a response in those old days'. Eventually the sun set, the tall brass Florentine lamps were lit, the roses began to release their scent and the guests drifted off through the fourteenth-century *cortile* and disappeared in their carriages, down the cypress-lined avenue lit by the flickering flames of burning torches held by strong-armed servants.

The event – probably a rather more elegant version of the typical Anglo-Florentine garden-party – was a dramatic success, but Luhan recorded of her guests: 'I could have them if I want them. But I never really did…'. Although Nicky Mariano recalls her as having a typically American aura of 'boundless optimism', perhaps Mabel Dodge Luhan was simply too rich, or too avant-garde to appeal to the Anglo-Florentines.

While her confrères tended to concentrate on the past, attracting scholars, critics and historians, Luhan took her inspiration from the Medici and courted the stars of the moment, becoming an early advocate of psychoanalysis and Eastern philosophy while gathering around her such luminaries as actress Eleanor Duce, writer André Gide, photographer Carl Van Vechten, poet Mina Loy, political anarchist Emma Goldman and photographer Alfred Steiglitz. Arthur Rubenstein performed in the villa and in 1912, before her jealous companion Alice Toklas squashed the friendship, the impenetrable Gertrude Stein wrote one of her famous word portraits of Luhan, described as 'a cubist word-picture in verse'. The grateful sitter had an edition of 300 copies privately printed and bound in colourful Florentine wallpaper to present to honoured guests. Stein begins her *Portrait of Mabel Dodge at Villa Curonia* in her characteristically opaque style: 'The days are wonderful and the nights are wonderful and the life is pleasant', and ends it, just as perplexingly: 'That is what is done when there is done what is done and the union is won and the division is the explicit visit. This is not all of any visit.' Stein's brother Leo summed up their hostess rather more succinctly as 'Mabel Dodge, Hodge Podge'.

Like her fellow Anglo-Florentines Luhan had a penchant for al fresco entertaining. While her women guests were served trays in their bedrooms, Luhan insisted on breakfasting under the roses in her pergola as her manservant, the devoted Domenico, hovered with strong coffee and steaming milk. She recounts many memorable meals on the gravel terrace beneath the branches of an old ilex tree, the narrow table covered with coarsely woven cloth and hand-made pottery. Of one particularly notable evening she recalls: 'In the twilight, with flagons of wine and a round loaf at each plate and the blossoms sprinkled here and there, it was like a picture of the Last Supper before the Disciples sat down.' She goes on to describe the yellow candlelight, black ilex leaves silhouetted against the moon and Gertrude Stein, 'spreading through the openings in her chair'.

After eight years of the Anglo-Florentine villa fantasy, Luhan got bored. She shed her second husband, dabbled in American politics, had an affair with the labour activist John Reed, then turned to collecting modern art and contracting a brief marriage to the painter Maurice Sterne. Finally she exchanged old world sophistication for new world spirituality and settled in Taos, New Mexico, where she wrote her autobiography while continuing to act as a hostess and patron, enticing such luminaries as D.H.Lawrence, Georgia O'Keefe and Ansel Adams to settle in the remote region. She also became involved in Indian affairs and in 1926 married a local Pueblo Indian, Tony Luhan, who sported native dress and two long, black braids.

This marriage, Luhan's fourth, lasted until her death in 1962. According to Harold Acton, Jacques-Emile Blanche, who had once painted her resplendent in Renaissance dress in the Villa Curonia, concluded: 'In the arms of a Mexican Indian, Tony Luhan, she found the answer to the enigma, and at Taos the primeval country for which her soul thirsted – or so it seems.'

RIGHT *Jacques-Emile Blanche,* Mabel Dodge, *c.1913. Bernard Berenson once noted that Luhan befriended 'all the people in Florence whom we consider undesirable'. Unlike most of her confrères she eventually tired of the Anglo-Florentine fantasy and drifted back to America where she exchanged her Renaissance costumes for socialist politics and avant-garde art.*

13
A scholar's haven
BERNARD BERENSON'S I Tatti

For a century I Tatti owed its fame largely to its owner, the brilliant art historian Bernard Berenson. Recently, however, the estate has attracted attention because of Cecil Pinsent, the architect whose first major project was to transform this simple farmhouse into an elegant villa and garden.

Berenson arrived in Florence in 1888 with a Harvard degree and a commission from his patron, Isabella Stewart Gardner, to acquire Italian art for her private collection. As a young art historian he realised he would never penetrate the American art establishment, being triply disqualified by his Jewish ancestry, his Lithuanian origins and his liaison with a married woman, Mary Costelloe – a noted scholar in her own right and sister-in-law to the philosopher Bertrand Russell. Berenson's best chance for success was in the cosmopolitan atmosphere of Europe, and he was drawn particularly to Florence with its huge store of Renaissance art.

Like Arthur Acton, Berenson built up his own collection and dealt discreetly in art while advising private collectors and public galleries. He also, controversially, attributed paintings for dealers. Following the work of the Italian scholar Giovanni Morelli, Berenson evolved a scientific method of stylistic analysis. Focusing on the paintings themselves rather than their provenance – written documentation and anecdotal evidence – he examined such technical details as the brushstroke or the treatment of eyes, ears, hands and drapery. By building up a physiological profile of the artist, Berenson could offer more accurate attributions than had previously been possible. In later years his credibility was undermined by the revelation that from 1912 he had accepted a generous retainer from the dealer, Joseph Duveen. Nonetheless Berenson's recovery and promotion of early Renaissance artists virtually created the market for their works, which hitherto, through lack of exposure and the inability to authenticate, had been virtually nonexistent.

Berenson first rented I Tatti in 1900, after the death of her Catholic husband freed his paramour to marry him; they finally legitimised their union at Janet Ross' Poggio Gherardo, where Berenson stayed as a guest while his villa was being made habitable.

I Tatti's unusual name is probably a corruption of Zatti, the sixteenth-century owners of the farm. In the late nineteenth century the estate was one of many on the hillside purchased by John Temple Leader; his double 'L' monograph still adorns the main gate. By 1907 Berenson's immense success enabled him to purchase I Tatti from Temple Leader's impecunious heir, Lord Westbury. Twenty-eight thousand dollars bought him the main house, outbuildings, several farms and fifty acres of land.

Like most Anglo-Florentines, the Berensons demanded a greater degree of comfort than their Italian forebears, so they set about altering the villa. From small beginnings – an upstairs bathroom for Mary and a library for BB (as he was widely known) – the alterations multiplied. In her effort to keep Berenson's young librarian, Geoffrey Scott, nearby, Mary convinced Cecil Pinsent to form a partnership with Scott. She then kept the pair employed with an ever-extending list of projects, including a gardener's house, a new staircase, corridors and wings for the villa, all of which Berenson furnished with exquisite discretion, ensuring nothing distracted from his magnificent early Renaissance paintings. Young and inexperienced, the partnership – which Mary dubbed 'The Firm', or 'The Infirm' when they were out of favour – was slow, sloppy and inefficient, incurring enormous cost overruns which Mary had to disguise from her irascible husband.

Though Berenson modestly described his villa as 'a library with rooms attached', others felt it soon became too opulent for its setting. Berenson's assistant Nicky Mariano, who lived in an extraordinary ménage with the Berensons, attributes the aggrandisement of the villa to Mary, adding that the original farmhouse better suited Berenson's 'conservative nature'. Within three years the renovation costs had exceeded $100,000 and friends began referring to the estate as 'BB's folly'. But when the villa was finished, Mary moved on to the grounds.

While I Tatti's gardens are often attributed to Berenson, Pinsent seems the most likely designer, although there is little evidence as to who, in fact, came up with the final design. As The Firm was virtually living on site, most discussions were conducted face to face, and any formal documentation was disposed of in Pinsent's regular purging of his papers. Nonetheless in November 1909 Aubrey Waterfield, in a letter to his wife, claims: 'Pinsent has already drawn a plan for the garden and he professes where plants are to go.' (Indeed, unknown to Pinsent, Mary had hired the unfortunate Waterfield, who thought he was going to design the whole garden and ended up simply planting the meadow.) The letters in the archive suggest that the garden, like the villa restoration, was Mary's idea. Some believe Berenson only discovered a garden was being planned when Scott unwittingly showed him the designs during Mary's absence, though it is unlikely that the project could have proceeded very far without his approval.

When the First World War was declared, Berenson, as an American, was deemed neutral, nonetheless, at the onset of the hostilities he abandoned the Germanic spelling of his name Bernhard. Soon after, he and Mary retreated to England, leaving Pinsent to oversee the renovations. Writing to Mary, Pinsent reveals the difficulty of working in wartime, explaining that cheques are uncashable, there is no money to pay the workers and he is preparing to lock up the treasures lest refugees commandeer the villa. Nonetheless the work continued and Berenson's friends Sybil Cutting and Charles Strong both gave the young architect work, helping him survive the war years.

The grounds at I Tatti were a difficult commission for a novice designer as the villa is awkwardly sited in steep agricultural land, halfway down a sloping hillside. Before the renovations the building was a well-proportioned farmhouse rising above a small lemon garden, enclosed to the south with a *limonaia* in which the Berensons took their afternoon tea. To the east, a line of cypresses had been stranded when the main road was moved in the late nineteenth century to lessen the grade of the slope.

ABOVE AND BELOW *Enclosed in a letter to his wife who was visiting Poggio Gherardo, Aubrey Waterfield's sketch reveals how the* limonaia *separated the villa from the slope below. Cecil Pinsent brilliantly transformed the steep, awkward site into an elegant terraced enclosure.*

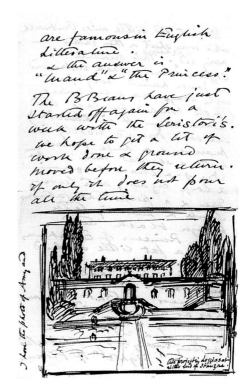

Pinsent added a parallel line of cypresses to create a shady walk from the villa down to the old entrance gate at the bottom of the property. Balancing this, on the west side of the villa, he designed an ornate baroque terrace off the library, with an elaborate wall fountain and a parterre of low box beds.

It is in the formal garden at the front of the villa, however, that Pinsent's work is most evident. Here he transformed the sloping lemon garden into a wide terrace with two levels of flanking beds to satisfy Mary's longing for flowers. Beyond the long, horizontal *limonaia*, Pinsent created the Green Garden, a formal, stepped half-acre space surrounded by tall cypress hedges.

With his dramatic juxtaposing of sun and shade, open and closed spaces, formality and naturalism, Pinsent imitated his early Renaissance forebears, exploring the intersection of the man-made and the natural. By terracing the rocky slope, he created four shallow parterres descending to a pair of still pools. Each parterre is enclosed within double hedges and filled with symmetrical pairs of low box borders. The drop from the *limonaia* is bridged by a double staircase curving round a niche filled with the unlikely image of Our Lady. This pious statue is flanked by a winsome stonework puppy and kitten carrying baskets of fruit – which must have been a gift that the Berensons felt obliged to display as nothing else can explain such an incongruously kitsch addition to this austere, intellectual space.

A second double staircase leads from the Green Garden to a small ilex wood. Although originally designed to screen the farmhouse behind, today the trees are cut low so as not to obscure the countryside beyond. Bisecting the Green Garden a central axis runs through the curved arch of the *limonaia*, linking the formal villa above to the informal woodland below.

With its Baroque façade, vibrant flower beds, Renaissance parterres, grass walks, formal forest and flowery meadows, Pinsent's design could be condemned as incoherent. Or it could simply reveal the young architect's inability to control the egos competing to shape the space, as Mary fought for English exuberance and Berenson for Italian austerity.

As Pinsent's first attempt at garden making in the Italian style, I Tatti has provoked various responses. While some praise its variety and charm, others, like the art historian Kenneth Clark – who, in his youth served briefly as Berenson's librarian – condemned it as pompous and vulgar. Clark felt the scale of the garden was too grand for the house, although the garden he saw was in its infancy; as it matured, the low hedges became high enclosures, the lines of trees became shaggy woodland, the proportions shifted and the garden settled harmoniously into the surrounding landscape.

In the late 1920s Rose Nichols described I Tatti as having 'a particularly delightful atmosphere'. Her observation that 'both Mr and Mrs Berenson have a keen sense of beauty that finds expression in their immediate environment' suggests that at that time Mary's contribution to the design was acknowledged. Several decades later in his *Tuscan Villas*, Harold Acton is less effusive, claiming of the design, 'its Tuscan elements have been cleverly adapted rather than absorbed. The scale as well as the dainty precision of the details is more English than Florentine.' Such faint praise may stem from the fact that I Tatti rivalled his own La Pietra as the most glittering jewel in the Anglo-Florentine crown.

While his work at I Tatti forced Pinsent to study the classical style demanded by his patrons, it also enabled the young architect to explore the monumental, pared down formality which would become his hallmark. The Berensons were generous patrons and even when I Tatti was finished they promoted Pinsent's career by

BELOW *Bernard Berenson and Mary Costelloe courting in 1893 when she was still married to a Catholic barrister and he was an unknown American scholar.*

encouraging friends to employ him. In 1911 Sybil Cutting hired Pinsent to modernise her Villa Medici, Fiesole, then to restore and extend the garden. In 1913 Charles Strong, commissioned Pinsent to design a hillside villa, and in 1924 Cutting's newly married daughter, Iris Origo, asked Pinsent to help develop her estate in the Val d'Orcia.

Though he did many other projects over the years, these commissions form the bulk of his work and through them he evolved his distinctive modern villa style. In 1945, before being demobbed, Pinsent wrote to Berenson at I Tatti, claiming:

> I owe you a debt of gratitude – you and Mary, that is; for it was you who brought me to Italy and started me off (having exercised a great deal of 'pazienza' I know) and made possible 28 happy years spent in this country, of which I would not wish to change a day.

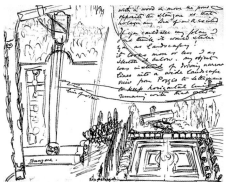

LEFT AND ABOVE *This aerial view of I Tatti shows the variety of garden spaces: the cypress-lined walk to the right and the wild-flower meadow to the left flank Pinsent's 'Green Garden', which links the* limonaia *and flower borders on the top terrace with the woodland* bosco *at the bottom. Waterfield's sketch shows the evolution of the design.*

ABOVE *The Baroque Garden. Berenson's spirit lives on at I Tatti where today's scholars enact the same rituals as punctuated the master's day, with study in the library relieved by pre-prandial drinks on the garden terrace, post-prandial coffee in the Baroque Garden and meditative strolls through the parterres of the Green Garden.*

Berenson himself was delighted with Pinsent's work. Writing at the end of his life, in his *Sketch for a Self-Portrait*, he revealed that he loved the garden 'as much as one can love any object or complex of objects not human', adding later, 'though I have travelled all over the world and seen many lovely places I now feel all the beauty I need is in my own garden'.

Although its owners' increasing fame and fortune preserved the villa through the two world wars, in 1940, when Italy joined the war on the Axis side, the Berensons were among the many Anglo-Florentines who had to flee for their own safety. In his diary Berenson noted: 'of all the improbabilities that could have been suggested when I first trod its earth in September 1888 none would have seemed more fantastic than that in my lifetime Italy would be at war with the United States'.

Though there had been little anti-Semitism in Italy since 1439 when the Signoria decreed that every Jew must wear a yellow badge, Berenson felt doubly vulnerable as a Jew and an American. He and Nicky Mariano went into hiding in a villa near Careggi, while Mary, too sick to move, remained at I Tatti. She was looked after by Mariano's sister, who courageously stored some of Berenson's most valuable treasures in her apartment in Florence. Mary was not alone in staying on; as Franco Zeffirelli depicted in his autobiographical film *Tea with Mussolini*, the Anglo-Florentine community contained many indomitable women who had become so entrenched in the region that when the British consulate attempted to repatriate them they refused to leave, preferring the risk of concentration camp to the idea of returning to England or America where they no longer had any ties.

When Mary Berenson died in 1945, Berenson, who had spent his whole adult life in the region, moved back to I Tatti in the care of Nicky Mariano. His diary notes rather wistfully:

> my favourite haunts for nearly half a century…have been sown by the Germans with mines, and wayfarers have lost their lives. Walks must be limited to the high road winding steeply past Vincigliata to the hilltop above – a little arduous for my eighty years.

In 1949 Berenson was made an honorary citizen of Florence; he spent the final decade of his life receiving an endless stream of distinguished visitors. Dubbed by Harold Acton 'the Sage of Settignano', Berenson epitomised the best of the Anglo-Florentines: a scholar, a connoisseur, a cosmopolitan exile, he loved all things Tuscan. On his death in 1959, he was buried next to Mary in the small chapel at I Tatti. Ignoring his wife's plea that he leave I Tatti to her children, Berenson bequeathed the estate to Harvard University so that it could continue as a centre of scholarly research. Harvard has maintained the villa impeccably, and through its various residency and seminar programmes I Tatti continues to inspire generations of Renaissance scholars.

14
A philosopher's retreat
CHARLES STRONG'S Le Balze

ABOVE *The atheist son of a Baptist minister, Charles Strong studied philosophy at Harvard under the pioneering psychologist William James. This is one of four busts, representing the philosophers Aristotle, Socrates, Demosthenes and Zeno, which embellish the grotto opposite the villa's front entrance.*

OPPOSITE *A simple enclosed garden sits beneath the loggia of Strong's bedroom.*

PINSENT'S SECOND MAJOR HORTICULTURAL PROJECT, and his only complete house and garden in Italy, is the villa he created for the American philosopher Charles Strong. Le Balze (the Bluffs) is named for the cliff on which it is situated. Despite the steep, narrow site Pinsent combined classical formality with English modesty to create a series of buttressed terraces, supporting two formal gardens, a grotto, a *bosco* or woodland and a large olive grove.

Yet another eccentric, Italophile outcast, Charles Strong (1862–1940) proved an ideal client. The atheist son of a Baptist minister, he had married John D.Rockefeller's daughter Bessie, who died in 1906 leaving him immensely wealthy and utterly desolate, with a nine year old daughter to care for. Retreating to Italy, Strong found solace in Fiesole's fourteenth-century San Girolamo monastery, where Michael Ondaatje moors the mysterious protagonist of his 1992 Booker prize-winning novel *The English Patient*. Five centuries earlier, Cosimo de' Medici had been so enraptured by the countryside around the monastery that he had purchased the adjacent property for his Villa Medici. Similarly enchanted, Strong bought a barren plot below the monastery, a vertiginous strip of land with spectacular views of the Arno valley. On the advice of his Harvard friend, Bernard Berenson, Strong hired the twenty-seven year old Pinsent to design and build him a simple villa. Like Michelozzi before him, Pinsent moved tons of earth and built immense retaining walls to support the villa and contain the reservoirs which would be needed to water the gardens through the long Italian summers.

Like I Tatti, Le Balze looks to the early Renaissance ideal, celebrating the harmony between man and nature. The simple parterres are filled with grass rather than colourful gravel or exotic plants; statuary is minimal and water effects are simple. Unlike his Renaissance forebears however, Pinsent hid the spectacular views behind tall yew hedges, cutting apertures into the greenery so the landscape beyond is revealed in tantalising glimpses.

Another deviation from the traditional formula is in the approach. Where Renaissance villas were generally approached from below to display the elegance of the architecture and its relationship to the landscape, the narrowness of the site forced Pinsent to put the main entrance at the back of the villa. Here a small service gate enters from the rural path above while a grander public entrance leads from the main road, via a raised, wisteria-clad pergola. Crowded against the slope of the hill the pergola extends to a double staircase which descends to the level of the villa. An experienced architect might have devised a more comfortable entrance, but Pinsent's elevated walk provides drama and variety as glimpses of distant countryside alternate with intimate views of the garden below.

LEFT *An arched opening in the garden off Strong's study frames the sculpture of a mysterious, cloaked philosopher at the end of the ilex wood.*

For the central dwelling Pinsent created a simple Palladian villa, flanked on each side by formal gardens, with a narrow front terrace opening onto the spectacular 180 degree panorama. To the east, overlooked by Strong's bedroom loggia, is the *giardino segreto* – a square space round a circular pool with a large potted camellia in the central island. Jasmine provides scent, while pots of azaleas and camellias offer seasonal colour.

To the west, leading off Strong's study, is an austere green garden enclosed by high hedges and bisected by paths. A small opening cut in the corner reveals the panoramic view from the front terrace, while an arch at the end leads to the formal woodland beyond. Similar to the *bosco* Pinsent had recently created at I Tatti, this ordered arrangement of evergreen ilexes suggests the groves of classical philosophers, a nod to the owner's profession.

By 1919 Strong was confined to a wheelchair, so when the property to the east came up for sale he acquired it to allow direct access to the villa from the Via Vecchia Fiesolana – the old Fiesole road. Once again Strong commissioned Pinsent to design the new entrance and rethink the journey round the grounds. In the newly acquired space Pinsent designed a formal Orange Garden with potted citrus trees enclosing a forum created from high, pleached trees. The *villino* on the site was turned into a *limonaia* for over-wintering the citruses, while its flat roof formed a loggia for the old entrance above.

In the Orange Garden Pinsent made much use of *ciottolato*, a traditional paving technique in which complex patterns are created from coloured pebbles. Though he had first used it to decorate the central axis of I Tatti's Green Garden, at Le Balze Pinsent employed *ciottolato* to line a grotto at one end, to form an urn at the other and, more traditionally, to create a vibrant ground surface. It was at this time that Pinsent also created the elaborate grotto at the base of the staircase from the upper pergola. Sited opposite the villa's main entrance, the grotto humidifies the air while filling the central hall with sparkling light and the cooling sound of water. The playful exuberance of these later additions seems at odds with the austerity of the rest of the grounds; nearly a decade after creating the original gardens, Pinsent appears to have broken out, adding a touch of whimsy to the austere, intellectual villa.

Le Balze demonstrates Pinsent's increasing ability to manipulate awkward space. Inspired, no doubt, by the example of the Villa Medici next door, he transformed a steep narrow site to create a harmonious relationship between dwelling, gardens and surrounding landscape, integrating the villa into the historic slope through a series of contrasting spaces – open and closed, long and short, intimate and distant.

BELOW *Le Balze's narrow top terrace provides spectacular panoramas of the city below. Geoffrey Jellicoe described Pinsent as 'a master' in the art of placing buildings in the landscape.*

Below the main terrace, a less formal garden incorporates palms, bamboo, agave and other fashionable exotics. Beneath this, hay fields are filled with peach, lilac, willow and Judas trees, giving way to olive groves punctuated with towering cypresses. These stately emblems of divinity contrast with the mundane olive trees, continuing the dialogue between wilderness and civilisation, chaos and order, the sacred and the profane, which animates the garden above.

Though Strong could have bought any number of existing Renaissance villas, his decision to build something new suggests a shift in the Anglo-Florentine attitude; rather than simply buying a chunk of the past Strong commissioned something new and of its time, neither recreation nor restoration, nor indeed, pastiche. This provided an extraordinary opportunity for Pinsent to develop his style. Tempering classical formality with modernist simplicity he created a modest, varied, ordered, evergreen space.

Though Strong was remarkably generous in his youth – at Harvard he once shared a $1,000 scholarship with the impecunious fellow student George Santayana – during his years in Italy he became increasingly isolated. The American stock market crash reduced his income from $25,000 to a mere $5,000 per annum, and Santayana, a frequent guest, complained that his host refused him a second glass of wine at dinner. By the late 1930s Strong's finances were restored and Santayana joyfully reported that the furnace was running full blast and they were 'tutti contenti'.

BELOW *This exuberant grotto, housing a water-spitting Triton, is tucked into the staircase linking the villa to the entrance above.*

ABOVE *With the villa set on a narrow outcrop in the steep olive terraces, Pinsent was still able to incorporate several walled gardens, an ilex wood and a grotto into the estate, which was linked to the main road by this wisteria-covered entrance pergola.*

Unlike many of his compatriots, Strong was wary of the pernicious influence of Mussolini, whom he considered 'evil'. Encouraging a young philosophy student to return to America while it was still possible to do so, he commented 'Santayana and Berenson and I are old men…it is all very well for us to stick it out here in Italy'. In 1940, just before Italy entered the Second World War, Charles Strong died in the villa, with only his house servant and chauffeur for company. Despite his loneliness, depression and general misanthropy, he endowed several philosophy fellowships before his death.

During the war Le Balze was requisitioned as the head office for the Bank of Tuscany, before being taken over by the German military. Although they wilfully damaged the neighbouring convent of San Girolamo, the occupying forces treated the villa with remarkable respect. It survived unscathed until 1944 when allied bombs destroyed parts of the villa, *villino*, garden wall and various trees. During a spell in Florence as an officer of the British Army's Monuments, Fine Arts and Archive Commission, Pinsent managed to visit Le Balze and was able to advise on repairs.

After the war the property remained uninhabited until 1979 when Georgetown University purchased it from Strong's daughter. Today, as the centre of Georgetown's European Studies programme, Le Balze continues to be a philosopher's garden, housing America's academic elite. With its classical lines, human scale and contemporary simplicity, it is one of the most elegant of the Anglo-Florentine villas.

15
A humanist garden
SYBIL CUTTING'S Villa Medici, Fiesole

ABOVE *Sybil Cutting poses in her wedding dress in the villa's celebrated salon with its yellow eighteenth-century Chinese silk wallpaper.*

OPPOSITE *The Villa Medici dominates the Fiesole hillside, framed by the ubiquitous cypress and olive trees, which represent, respectively, eternity and seasonal fertility.*

WHILE OVERSEEING THE CONSTRUCTION OF LE BALZE, Cecil Pinsent was invited to help with the restoration of the Villa Medici across the road. Celebrated as the first purpose-built humanist dwelling, the villa featured large in the Anglo-Florentine imagination, especially as much of its history had been passed in the ownership of English expatriates.

Unlike the other Medici villas of a similar date, such as Cafaggiolo and Il Trebbio, Villa Medici was not developed as part of an agricultural estate, nor was it adapted from a pre-existing building. Conceived as a suburban dwelling solely for intellectual and artistic pursuits, the villa was commissioned in the mid fifteenth century by Cosimo the Elder for his son Giovanni. Designed by Michelozzi, it dominates the hillside like a large, white cube, proclaiming the humanist fascination with geometry. Breaking from the medieval model of defensive, inward-looking dwellings clustered around an open courtyard, the Villa Medici dispensed with the courtyard altogether and faced outward instead, focusing on the landscape beyond. At its centre was a grand salon with a loggia at each end, inserted into the volume of the building, to absorb the countryside right into the body of the dwelling. Murals on the salon walls depicting the surrounding landscape further drew the outside in while celebrating nature as the pagan world had done.

Although the site itself was chosen for its panoramic views, the feat of inserting a large building into the sloping hillside was an engineering triumph celebrated for centuries to come. Indeed Vasari later described the villa as 'a splendid and noble palace', explaining that its foundations were sunk at very great expense into the rock to create the cellars, storerooms and stables essential to any gentleman's residence. Perched on the cliff edge, the villa certainly offered magnificent views of Florence and the surrounding hills. Nonetheless, although it satisfied Alberti's maxim that a villa should overlook a city or plain 'bounded by familiar mountains', with a 'delicacy of gardens' in the foreground, the precarious site did not find favour with everyone. In 1779, after dining at the villa, the English traveller Henry Swinburne complained that it was 'too high, too much confined and on a rock which reflects a burning heat in summer'.

With its celebration of nature and its elegant construction, the Villa Medici soon surpassed Careggi to become the favourite Medici dwelling. It was here, at a banquet in 1478, that the Pazzi family intended to assassinate their hosts, Cosimo's grandsons, Giuliano and Lorenzo. When the evening was cancelled after Giuliano suffered 'an inflammation of the eyes', the Pazzis struck the following morning in the cathedral. Giuliano was murdered, but his brother escaped to see the assassins executed.

The villa passed to Lorenzo and soon became the gathering place of the Platonic Academy, which numbered among its members the philosopher Marsilio Ficino and

LEFT *In the late fifteenth century Leonardo and his fellow neo-Platonists would meet in this loggia of the Villa Medici to conduct their discussions. Charles Latham's atmospheric 1905 photographs (see also pages 38/9) reveal the baroque polychrome decoration which Pinsent wished to remove. Although Sybil Cutting refused, the villa's current owners have returned the villa to its austere fifteenth-century purity.*

the poet Angelo Poliziano. As tutor to Lorenzo's sons, Poliziano composed his famous *Rusticus* at the villa. In a delightful letter he begs Ficino to join him:

> There is an abundance of water here, and, as we are on the edge of a valley, but little sun, and the wind is certainly never lacking. The villa itself lies off the road, in a dense wood, but commands a view of the whole city, and although the district is thickly populated I enjoy that solitude dear to those who have fled from town.

With the growing taste for baroque opulence, later generations grew less enchanted with the austere villa, and in 1671, soon after acceding to power, Cosimo III de' Medici sold it to the del Sera family for 4,000 florins. A century later, in 1772, the villa was purchased by an English aristocrat Lady Orford. After a brief marriage to Sir Robert Walpole's eldest son, this eccentric heiress left her husband and young child, settling in Florence where she accumulated lovers, dressed like a Venetian courtesan and plagued the English ambassador, Sir Horace Mann. When her profligate offspring faced ruin in England she refused to visit him, claiming age and infirmity, though the ambassador dryly observed, 'she rides for some hours every morning, and is in continual motion the rest of the day, by which she maintains a vivacity not common at her age'.

In 1780 Orford had the villa refurbished by the fashionable Italian architect Gasparo Paoletti. Overlaying the fifteenth-century simplicity with the rococo taste of the time, he introduced the famous Chinese yellow silk wallpaper so beloved of the later Anglo-Florentines. Less successfully, he extended the villa to the north to create staff quarters; this act of architectural desecration destroyed the serene symmetry of the original, lending it an uncomfortable, lopsided air. Outside, Paoletti moved the main entrance from the Via Vecchia Fiesolana to the recently constructed Via Beato Angelico. While his new carriage drive, winding through oak woodlands, made a more dramatic entrance, it altered the organisation of both villa and garden. To frame the views of the city, Paoletti added a belvedere to the left of the drive, a grotto-like structure, encrusted, externally, with decorative rockwork and embellished on the interior with whimsical *trompe l'oeil* murals depicting the entrance avenue behind.

Paoletti also added the elegant *limonaia* against the northern boundary wall so his client could over-winter her prized citruses. Until then any tender trees had been espaliered against the buttressing wall of the terrace, where they could absorb the sun's heat in clement weather while being protected from winter frosts by portable, lean-to shelters made of wickerwork or wooden slats. The *limonaia* allowed for the introduction of exotics such as *melaranci* or bitter oranges, as well as the delicate camellias and azaleas so prized in the late eighteenth century.

On her death, Lady Orford left the villa to her young lover, Cavalier Mozzi, who promptly married and sold the estate to a Sienese family. In the nineteenth century the property returned to the English community and was known as the Villa Spence after its owner, William Blundell Spence. Despite the change in name, it was still closely associated with its illustrious forebears; Lady Paget's diary records that she dined with Mr Spence 'at his Medicean villa', after which they sat 'on the terrace where the Pazzi had plotted against the lives of Lorenzo and Giulio di Medici'.

It is Spence who established the art-dealing tradition taken up by many in the following century. Drawn to Florence to study painting, Spence survived as a copyist in the galleries, supplementing his income by dealing in art, guiding English visitors around the city and effecting introductions to famous artists. In 1862, having married into the local aristocracy, Spence could afford to purchase the Villa Medici. In this illustrious setting he displayed his wares to newly rich visitors keen to acquire respectability by purchasing ancient artefacts; so successful was Spence in this enterprise that he soon acquired an international reputation.

A generous host and passable painter, Spence donated his self-portrait to the Uffizi and wrote a popular guide to the city, *The Lions of Florence*. In 1865 he widened the entrance avenue of the Villa Medici to suit the larger carriages of the time; when a section of Etruscan wall was revealed during the works, the event was duly noted in the local English-language *Athenaeum* magazine. Spence himself celebrated the find by erecting a plaque to record the occasion.

Upholding the tradition of hospitality associated with the villa, in 1866 Spence invited the newly married painter William Holman Hunt to spend his honeymoon in the villa, providing him with a studio above the carriage house. In 1848 Holman Hunt and Dante Gabriel Rosetti had been among the founders of the Pre-Raphaelite Brotherhood, inspired by their shared fascination for Florence's early, primitive painters. During his honeymoon Holman Hunt painted a portrait of his pregnant wife Fanny in medieval mode, posed against a fireplace in a richly decorated room – probably the salon of the Villa Medici. In another, equally medieval depiction, she poses as Keats' Isabella with her pot of basil. Sadly Fanny died later that year in childbirth; she was buried in the English cemetery beside Elizabeth Barrett Browning. Her tomb, sculpted by her husband, resembles an elegant classical sarcophagus resting on a cushion of marble waves.

After Spence's death in 1897, the villa was purchased by Colonel Harry Macalmon, an enigmatic figure whose only adjustment to the property was to increase the height of

BELOW *Domenico Ghirlandaio, detail from* The Dormition of the Virgin *(see page 104). The villa's steep buttressing walls are evident in this detail, which also depicts the monks at the San Girolamo monastery behind – a subtle pairing of religion and wealth. Giovanni Tornabuoni, who commissioned the painting for his family chapel, managed the Medici bank in Genoa; the inclusion of the celebrated villa pays homage to his powerful employers while attesting to his own humanist ideals.*

the northern boundary walls to ensure greater privacy. Although there are few descriptions of the garden in this period, Lady Paget cryptically records a visit as 'one glow of giant chrysanthemums'. In 1905 Charles Latham was too enchanted with the villa's humanist connections to comment on its current state, but he did provide photographs of the eastern front which show the loggia brightly painted with baroque polychrome decorations on the outer walls, Roman grotesques on the inner walls and pots of flowers clustered round the columns.

This early twentieth-century image was much more exuberant than the austere, historically accurate façade presented today; even at the time, however, Mabel Luhan found the villa uncomfortably severe: 'the rigid symmetry, the proportion of height to length and breadth prohibited grace and ease in spite of its stately elegance'. Although she was looking for a dwelling to inhabit all year round, ultimately Luhan eschewed the south-facing villages of Fiesole and its neighbour Settignano, claiming the villas were too close together: 'all looking down on each other's red-tiled roofs and terraces and gardens from where they perched on the steep hillside'.

Eventually, however, the Villa Medici was rented by another young heiress, the Anglo-Irish aristocrat Lady Sybil Cutting. Cutting arrived in Florence in 1910 as a grieving widow. Her husband, the diplomat Bayard Cutting, had been sent to Milan in 1908 as American vice consul, where he was charged with delivering Red Cross aid to the victims of the recent earthquake in Messina. A year later he died suddenly of tuberculosis while holidaying on the Nile. His widow remained in Europe to fulfil her husband's deathbed wish that she raise their daughter abroad. With uncanny prescience Bayard Cutting anticipated that nationalism would be the scourge of the budding century and in his final letter he begged his wife to bring up their child 'somewhere she does not belong', so she could avoid the snare of patriotism and be free to love 'anyone she likes, of any country'.

Though keen to inhabit a venerable dwelling, Cutting was also mindful of her health, so she looked to the sunny, south-facing villas on the hills north of the city. When Cutting first rented the property in 1911 it had hardly changed since the eighteenth century; the villa itself contained five bedrooms, a chapel and a separate cottage, known, as such appendages often were, as Il Villino – the little villa. In her autobiography *Images and Shadows*, Cutting's daughter, Iris Origo, described her introduction to the villa as a magical drive up the road to Fiesole, where high walls tangled in wisteria and roses alternated with open views of terraced olive groves. They turned down a long, ilex-shadowed drive to discover the villa – 'a square house with a deep loggia looking due west towards the sunset over the whole valley of the Arno'. This became her home until her marriage fourteen years later, and 'certainly no child could have had a more beautiful one'.

Reinstating its earlier name of Villa Medici, Cutting purchased the estate a few years later and set out to restore it, encouraged no doubt by Bernard Berenson, already the doyenne of the community and soon to become her lover. In that incestuous community their relationship passed almost without notice; even the cuckolded Mary greeted it with relief, noting to a friend that Sybil was a great improvement on her husband's previous mistress, John Pierpont Morgan's librarian, Belle de Costa Greene.

As one of the treasured *Americani con soldi* – Americans with money – Cutting was welcomed by local antique dealers and sought out by the middlemen who acted for impoverished nobles. Filling her rooms with rococo mirrors, primitive paintings, baroque furniture and antique textiles, she also discreetly inserted such modern conveniences as indoor plumbing and heating. Inspired by his work at Le Balze next door

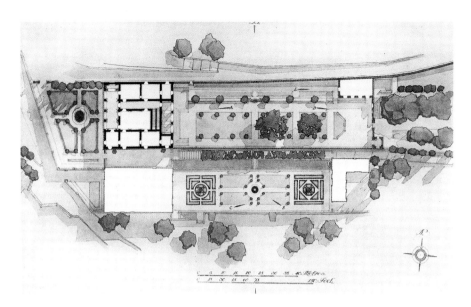

and with a recommendation from Berenson, Cutting hired Cecil Pinsent to oversee her renovations. This commission honed Pinsent's style and established his reputation as the designer best able to interpret Renaissance traditions for a modern anglophone clientele.

When the interior was finished Pinsent moved on to the grounds. Though simple in design, the gardens extended over several of the former agricultural terraces. Fifteenth-century illustrations show a single lawn stretching out from the ground floor loggia with a lower grassy strip against the steep buttressing wall. While later Renaissance designers soon learned to exploit such steep sites with grand ramps and staircases, at the Villa Medici the lower level is accessible only by an interior staircase through the cellars, by steep steps from the south side of the villa or by a circuitous route from the later western entrance.

By Cutting's day the top terrace consisted of a large rectangular lawn divided into three sections, punctuated with potted lemons and dominated by two huge *Paulownia tomentosa*. Thirteen feet below, beside the enormous buttressing wall, Pinsent laid out a simple, parallel garden with four rectangular grass parterres, punctuated by topiary cones, ranged round a central fountain. The intervening grassy strip he embellished with a pergola flanking the steps to the lower garden. In the turning circle of the former eighteenth-century entrance to the west, he created a third garden, sometimes known as the *giardino segreto*. Like the lower garden, this simple geometric space has a humanist flavour with its plain box-edged beds surrounding an elegant oval fountain.

Origo's autobiography reveals that even though the villa was virtually a suburb of Florence, it retained a picturesque rural quality. She recalls how, breaking free from her governesses, she would escape to the dark ilex wood above the formal gardens, or beyond to the steep terraces of the *podere*, part of it cultivated with wheat, part abandoned to long grass and little pink Tuscan roses. In true Anglo-Florentine fashion she extols the great stone blocks of the Etruscan wall and refers to an Etruscan well hidden deep in the woods.

Like her daughter, Sybil Cutting had a profound love of the Tuscan countryside; spurred on by Pinsent, who soon became a family friend, she engineered an exhausting round of garden parties, picnics and excursions. Tea on the lawn was a Sunday afternoon ritual; Kinta Beevor, Janet Ross' great niece, recalls a May Day party when she, as the youngest child, was paraded around on a throne before being crowned Queen of the May with an uncomfortable wreath of flowers. Origo describes summer balls on moonlit nights when the air was heavy with jasmine and roses, and fireflies darted in the surrounding wheat fields. After supper on the terrace, beneath Japanese lanterns, there would be music, dancing and fireworks which soared, 'like jewelled fountains'. For more intimate entertainments, Berenson would arrive, with his picnic-basket and chauffeur, to take her mother driving in the hills; there, all affectations abandoned, the great critic would leap around, exclaiming at a fading fresco in some remote country church, or gazing, wrapt, at a distant landscape: "'Look, a Corot' he would say, or 'a Perugino'."

Although a chronic hypochondriac, Sybil Cutting was also an intrepid tourist; while she normally travelled with an entourage of servants, friends and cumbersome comforts, she was just as happy to find herself alone in a remote desert oasis or mountain-top hermitage. Beevor saw her as a character 'straight out of a novel by Edith Wharton'. Acton described her as a determined intellectual: 'something of the Platonic Academy still lingered…'. Aldous Huxley thought her one of the 'brightest spots' among the city's intelligentsia, before rejecting her privileged lifestyle and creating a vicious portrait of her in his justly forgotten 1925 *Those Barren Leaves*. Here Cutting is presented as the self-centred Lillian Aldwinkle, an ambitious heiress whose £270,000 capital fund is built on the exploitation of others: 'at this very moment, men and women of every race and colour were doing their bit to supply Mrs Aldwinkle with her income….People worked; Mrs Aldwinkle led the higher life.'

Much admired if not much liked, Cutting was clearly both intelligent and courageous; she wrote an autobiography, a travel guide based on her peregrinations in Egypt, Syria and Palestine and a collection of fairy tales; she also edited an anthology about the sea which was published in 1918 by the Oxford Clarendon Press, but none of these efforts has survived the test of time. During the First World War she was one of many Anglo-Florentines who stayed on in Italy. From their lofty villas, the war was only a distant rumble. Some, like Harold Acton, celebrated the absence of tourists, which allowed him to explore the countryside and visit its treasures undisturbed. Cutting and her daughter delighted in entertaining convalescing officers, for whose company they competed with I Tatti, La Pietra and Villa Le Balze. While the women organised Red Cross fund-raisers, Pinsent and Geoffrey Scott, ensconced in their urban flat, rented a piano and hosted the sort of soirées formerly held by their patrons.

In 1917 Cutting unexpectedly married Geoffrey Scott, the ill-matched pair cleaving together against the destruction of their shared world. The marriage outraged the Berensons, depriving Bernard of his mistress and Mary of her swain. Several years later, still seeking a strong female figure to nurture his work, Scott began an ill-fated affair with Vita Sackville-West. Emerging soon after in a state of nervous collapse he quit Europe and moved to New York where, in 1929, he died, suddenly, of pneumonia.

By the end of the war Italy was exhausted and bankrupt; the lira was devalued, inflation skyrocketed, unemployment soared provoking crime, strikes and riots. Marauding gangs focused on the vulnerable hilltop villas, pillaging their cellars and stores; wine and whisky were stolen from I Tatti, maize and oil from Poggio Gherardo, but the presence of Cutting, as well as the prominent position of her dwelling, probably deterred the gangs from raiding the venerable Villa Medici.

In 1926, having divorced Geoffrey Scott, Cutting married the English literary critic Percy Lubbock and asked Aubrey Waterfield to find them a piece of land on the coast near his castle at Aulla. Waterfield found them a wooded promontory on a rocky bay at Lerici, jutting into the Gulf of Spezia – near the fisherman's cottage where, two decades earlier, D.H.Lawrence had written *The Rainbow*. In 1931 the Lubbocks commissioned Pinsent to design them a 'cottage'. The dwelling, which they named Gli Scafari, was a palatial villa with Carrara marble floors, silk-clad walls and a loggia overlooking the sea. Although it was originally intended simply as a summer retreat, the Lubbocks withdrew increasingly from the expatriate community and settled almost permanently in the privacy of Gli Scafari.

When the Second World War was declared the Lubbocks hung on in Italy; despite the advice of diplomats, family and friends. Finally, in June 1940, less than a week

RIGHT *Biagio di Antonio, detail from* The Annunciation, *c.1490 (Accademia di San Luca, Rome). The Villa Medici, framed by the loggia in Biagio's painting, perfectly fulfils Alberti's prescription that a gentleman's dwelling should be sited where it is highly visible, with vistas over gardens, plains, favourite hills, distant cities and the sea; it must be well supplied with roads to receive guests and it must have cooling breezes, shelter from the sun, woods for hunting and streams for fishing.*

before Italy joined on the Axis side, Origo secured them their visas and they fled to Switzerland. While the Swiss were hostile to refugees, demanding evidence of great wealth, genuine medical need or an onward ticket to another country, such affluent aristocrats as Sir George Sitwell, the Arthur Actons and Lady Lubbock were influential enough to secure refuge in that neutral country. On the evening before the Lubbocks left, Aubrey Waterfield – who had an even greater difficulty abandoning his adopted country – came over from Poggio Gherardo. He recalled how, unable to say goodbye, they lingered beneath the Chinese birds of the famous old wallpaper, 'neither knowing who or what would survive the impending chaos'.

Sybil was one of those who would not. Wasting away in Switzerland, she died in 1942. Her villa remained unscathed, although, after a vivid skirmish on the Fiesole hillside, Origo arrived in a Red Cross jeep to inspect the place and found a bomb-disposal squad busily at work. At the end of the war Lubbock could not bring himself to move back to Florence, and settled permanently at Gli Scafari. Origo considered keeping the villa but ultimately La Foce, the estate she had restored over thirty years, had a greater emotional pull and she sold the Villa Medici to the Mazzini family. They continue to inhabit it, maintaining the villa and gardens impeccably. Preserving the tradition of scholarship, they have produced an historic guide to the villa which they open, by appointment, to visiting scholars.

16
A baroque jewel
VILLA CAPPONI

OPPOSITE *Through the nineteenth and twentieth centuries the Villa Capponi housed such distinguished Americans as the Boston art historian Charles Perkins and Henry Clifford, curator of paintings at the Philadelphia Museum. In the early 1960s England's* Tatler *magazine claimed that Florence's summer season centred on the villa.*

A<small>LTHOUGH PINSENT'S WORK AT THE VILLA CAPPONI WAS RELATIVELY SMALL,</small> his adjustments to the overall design demonstrate the increasing elegance and subtlety of his approach. The villa had long been a favourite in the Anglo-Florentine community, indeed it contains one of the best preserved gardens in Italy, partly because it has had few owners over the centuries and those it has had were sensitive enough not to impose the passing whims of horticultural fashion on this baroque jewel. The oldest part of the building, the tower, probably dates from the fourteenth century, suggesting that the villa, like Paget's Torre de Bellosguardo nearby, began as a fortified farmhouse just beyond the city walls. The villa itself is sited on a southern hillside overlooking the Arno valley. Even today its steep surrounding slopes are covered with villas, vineyards and olive groves, reflecting that unique Tuscan combination of architectural refinement within an ordered agricultural setting, which Eberlein characterised as 'dignity and domestic repose'.

In 1572 Gino di Lodovico Capponi purchased the property. The Capponis were one of the richest and most powerful banking families in Florence and the family crest

RIGHT *A photograph by Harold Eberlein, c.1922, reveals how little the villa has changed. In 1905 Charles Latham described Capponi as 'one of the most charming English homes to be found on the Tuscan hills', adding that its garden, 'though small, is planned to the greatest advantage and is a dream of beauty in the spring-time'.*

still adorns the garden façade of the villa. It is likely that Lodovico Capponi began creating the pleasure gardens, transforming any existing herb or vegetable patches behind the dwelling into a long bowling green, inspired perhaps by that at the Villa Gamberaia north of the city – another Capponi property. While fulfilling Alberti's conviction that every garden should have an area for games, these stretches of lawn suggest that the early Italian gardener did appreciate the aesthetic value of turf even if large swathes of grass are not suited to the climate.

A lemon garden to the east and a secret garden to the west were probably created during the seventeenth century as their intricate, symmetrical beds and exuberant scroll-topped walls epitomise the baroque style. The lemon garden is separated from the lawn by a high wall adorned with a pair of terracotta lions bearing coats of arms; the pillars on the gate are further embellished with terracotta griffins. Although flower borders have infiltrated over the past few decades, the space is still divided into neat square and diamond parterres flanked by gravel paths. Potted citrus trees preside at the centre of each parterre, offset in spring with an informal planting of bright blue forget-me-nots. A dipping pool against the back wall allows for easy watering and the high enclosing walls, of the same golden hue as the villa, are topped with elegant terracotta urns. A nineteenth-century glass and iron *limonaia* sits outside the wall to the south, while to the north a dense planting of ilex and cypress trees suggest remnants of an earlier *ragnaia* or wilderness, demolished, no doubt, to create the formal garden.

At the western end of the lawn an intriguing *giardino segreto* is built into the slope of the hill one storey below the villa. A large, grilled window cut into the surrounding wall offers spectacular views over olive groves to the city below. This unusual feature reinforces the idea of the garden as an outdoor room, and indeed, until the twentieth century, it could only be entered from the house, via an underground passage through the cellars.

The villa remained in the Capponi family for three centuries being gradually enlarged and embellished as new rooms grew from the tower to form three sides of a

LEFT *Unusual terracotta griffons, bearing coats of arms, top the gateposts of the Lemon Garden adding an air of medieval fantasy to this classic Baroque villa. Coincidentally the griffon is the symbol of the Philadelphia Museum of Art, but as Eberlein's photograph attests, these griffons were guarding the garden before the Cliffords owned it.*

ABOVE *The lawn which stretches across the garden front at the Villa Capponi. Edith Wharton praised this 'fine oblong of old turf', suggesting it is the only surviving fragment of the original design.*

central courtyard with a curtain wall enclosing the fourth, separating the dwelling from the garden beyond. The layout of the villa demonstrates how intimately staff and master lived together in the past; the chapel, stable and servants' quarters are clustered to the east while the family rooms – adjoining the *cortile* or courtyard which provided light and fresh air – are gathered in the west. Only the central hall, leading directly from the street to the garden, separates the two spheres. Despite its luxurious gardens, the villa presents an austere façade to the public, being built right up against the steep, narrow road, onto which the chapel, stable and entrance doors all open directly.

In 1882 Lady Scott of Ancrum, daughter of the Duke of Portland and grandmother to the late queen mother, purchased the villa, bringing it into the Anglo-Florentine community, where it would remain for nearly a century. In 1905 Charles Latham described it as 'one of the most charming English homes to be found upon the Tuscan hills', adding that its garden was beautifully planted, presenting 'a dream of beauty', particularly in the spring.

A discreet character who barely features in the Anglo-Florentine gossip, Lady Scott was one of the first of the expatriates to exhibit respect for Italian horticultural tradition; happily her lead was followed by the subsequent owners. When Sir John Temple Leader was creating his gothic fantasies at Vincigliata and Georgina Grahame was stuffing her Italian garden with English flowers, Lady Scott demonstrated an unusual degree of restraint as she slipped her English additions seamlessly into the ancient fabric of the villa.

ABOVE AND LEFT *Originally this* giardino secreto *at the Villa Capponi was truly secret; located five metres below the level of the villa it was accessible only via a corridor from the villa's basement.*

It was probably Lady Scott who enlarged the bowling green to create the open lawn which provides an elegant foil to the architecture while linking the formal gardens with the countryside beyond. Harold Acton extolled this lawn as one of the best in Florence, 'a true *tapis vert'*. Keen to possess a rose garden, Lady Scott also carved a second walled enclosure lower down the western slope, accessed by a stone staircase from the *giardino segreto*. Here exuberant topiary scrollwork echoes the baroque swirls of the ancient walls; gravel paths and box-edged rose beds surround an oval fountain and a great yew hedge at on one end of the garden shelters three stone benches sited to enjoy the scent which must have been intoxicating within the high, sun-warmed walls.

It was probably also at this time that the underground passage from the house to the secret garden was turned into a rustic, tufa-lined grotto with a new stone staircase providing access from the lawn above. Lady Scott is probably also responsible for the roses which cover the pillars of the wrought-iron gate at the back of the villa. Framing the distant landscape of cypresses and olives, the pillars lead the eye from the ordered enclosure of lawn to the openness of the fields beyond.

In between restoring her villa, expanding her garden and hosting such illustrious visitors as Gertrude Jekyll and Queen Victoria, Lady Scott added the two loggias – one to the south, garden side and one to the west. Acton reports that she used to take tea in one and dinner in the other, the habit of dining al fresco being uniquely English at the time. Both loggias have an antique air because, like John Temple Leader, Lady Scott was quick to salvage the columns from Florence's medieval market when it was demolished in the late nineteenth century to make room for the Piazza della Repubblica.

The Price family from England acquired the property after Lady Scott's death, and in 1928 they sold it to Henry Clifford, curator of paintings at the Philadelphia Museum of Art and his wife, Esther, a medievalist. Associated, as it was, with both the English aristocracy and the Renaissance nobility, the Villa Capponi was bound to appeal to such cosmopolitan Americans. Soon after purchasing the estate the Cliffords hired Cecil Pinsent to modernise the villa and modify the garden. It is likely they met Pinsent through the Berensons with whom they were friendly, until a falling-out occurred, based, as Nicky Mariano records, 'on some silly gossip'.

Charged with inserting a swimming pool into the baroque design, Pinsent created a new garden room below Lady Scott's rose terrace, carving a space from the fields

RIGHT *Eberlein's plan of the Villa Capponi shows how masters and servants lived intimately, with servants crowded into the east side next to the chapel and stable, while the family's rooms, on the west, adjoined the courtyard with its light and fresh air; only a central hall leading from the street to the garden separated the two spheres.*

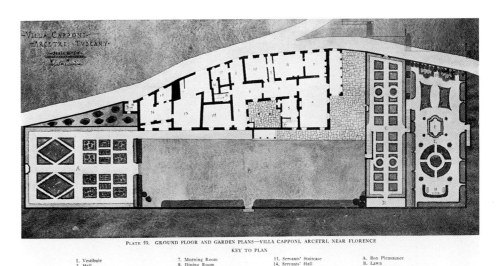

PLATE 59. GROUND FLOOR AND GARDEN PLANS—VILLA CAPPONI, ARCETRI, NEAR FLORENCE

KEY TO PLAN

1. Vestibule	7. Morning Room	13. Servants' Staircase
2. Hall	8. Dining Room	14. Servants' Hall
3. Inner Hall	9. Staircase	15. Coach House
4. Drawing Room	10. Library	16. Stable
5. Kitchen	11. Chapel	17. Box Stalls
6. Servants' Staircase	12. Sacristy	18. Outside Staircase

A. Box Pleasaunce
B. Lawn
C. Middle Garden
D. Lemon House
E. Lower Garden
F. Fountain and Pool

beyond the formal villa grounds. Playing on the theme of secret gardens he enclosed the pool with a tight cordon of high cypress hedges, interspersed, on the inside, with stone sculptures and marble benches. He then added water-spitting dolphins at either end transforming the utilitarian swimming pool into an elegant fountain (see page 37).

While providing privacy and screening the modern pool from the old garden, Pinsent's design also recalls the gymnasia of ancient Rome which provided athletes with swimming canals lined with inspirational sculptures. Pinsent also created a garden circuit, incorporating the country track which passes the pool garden, skirts the terraced lawn and leads past the *limonaia* at the eastern boundary. To create a harmonious link between the classical gardens and rural landscape, he planted the path with a formal line of cypresses along the villa side, and an informal line of lilacs, under-planted with irises and anemones abutting the field.

As the villa was one of several properties owned by the Cliffords, they never remained in Florence long enough to integrate with the expatriate community. During the war the villa succumbed to the fate of many such properties, being requisitioned, first by the Germans, then by the allies as they moved north sweeping the enemy out. Although the estate weathered the war largely unscathed, the first allied troops to arrive had to defuse a land mine in the front hall.

After the war the Cliffords spent less and less time at the villa, renting it to a stream of British and American tenants. In 1979, after Henry Clifford's death, the property was sold to the Benedetti family, who continue to preserve its character while inserting contemporary touches. When the roses succumbed to blight several years ago the rose garden was redesigned with wider, open gravel paths and the roses were replaced with circular parterres around large pots of plumbago, chrysanthemums and dahlias, reflecting the modern fashion for low maintenance, colour and longevity.

Though the gardens have been replanted over the centuries, the design of the Villa Capponi remains essentially Baroque, and while the estate ceased being a working farm in the nineteenth century, it still maintains 700 olive trees in the surrounding fields thus preserving the rural atmosphere so cherished by the ancients.

LEFT *Geoffrey Jellicoe described the swirling baroque walls of the western gardens at the Villa Capponi as 'so bubbling with fun that they chase away the cares of all who come'.*

OPPOSITE *The cavernous grotto at the Villa Capponi was created from the corridor that originally led from the villa providing the only access to the garden before a staircase was built from the lawn above.*

17

A modern pastoral in an ancient landscape
IRIS ORIGO'S La Foce

ABOVE *Iris Origo and her daughters Benedetta and Donata.*

OPPOSITE *The Fountain Garden, framed by the tall travertine gateposts which lead to the Lemon Garden beyond. To the right, tucked against the high wall that buttresses the flanking hillside, is an ingenious laurel arbour with a stone table and seat.*

IRIS ORIGO'S LA FOCE IS THE LAST, and in many ways the best, of the Anglo-Florentine villas. Created by an Anglo-American married to an Italian, it engaged with the land and the people of Tuscany in a way that few had done before; it also adapted to the changing economic and social conditions which ultimately destroyed the Anglo-Florentine community. In creating La Foce, Origo worked with Cecil Pinsent, her childhood friend, reprising the classic gender partnership in which he provided the architectural structure which she then clothed in colour, scent and texture.

Origo was an unusual woman; she lived through extraordinary times and responded with immense imagination, courage and compassion. Born in 1902 the only child of Bayard and Sybil Cutting, Origo had a cosmopolitan childhood travelling between her American grandparents in Long Island, her British grandparents in Kilkenny, the London home where her father acted as secretary to the American ambassador and long stretches at the Villa Medici.

Since her father's dying wish was that his daughter should be educated at home, Origo spent a lonely childhood in the company of her mother's intellectual Anglo-Florentine friends. When Pinsent came to design the garden at Villa Medici, despite the eighteen year age gap, he proved a godsend to the solitary child. On his death in 1963 Origo wrote to his family: 'he was, I think, my oldest friend; all the memories of childhood are mingled with him.'

At the time that Aldous Huxley was writing *Those Barren Leaves*, Origo was already rebelling against the insular community which he so viciously lampooned in his *roman-à-clef*. Ultimately she chose a more authentic Italian existence than any of her compatriots when, in 1924, she married a handsome, illegitimate, Catholic aristocrat, the Marchese Antonio Origo. In a situation worthy of a Henry James novel, he was impoverished, worldly and ten years older than the innocent heiress. Needless to say, her family attempted to stop the union. Bernard Berenson trekked down the hill from I Tatti to advise her to keep her American citizenship, while Mary Berenson confided to her diary: 'there is a sort of feeling abroad that she cannot be long happy with that anti-intellectual young man'. Having failed to prevent the marriage, Lady Cutting retreated to her sick bed and was absent from the wedding.

As predicted, the union was often strained, not least by his infidelities, her infidelities, the death, in childhood, of their beloved son and the political situation which left them with differing allegiances in the Second World War. Nonetheless the marriage survived and within it the Origos lived creative and productive lives. Spurred, perhaps, by the example of her indolent, hypochondriacal mother, the newly married Origo determined to do something useful. She envisioned social work, her husband had the instinctive Italian love of the land; they both wanted to leave the city, so, infused with Virgilian fantasies, they settled on a career in farming. Privately, Origo hoped for an austere villa with a long cypress-lined approach, a deep loggia, a courtyard, a well and a fountain garden surrounded by overgrown box hedges. Her husband wanted something more challenging.

On discovering that most of the available properties around Florence were already 'neat and fruitful', having been cultivated since the days of the *Decameron*, the Origos looked further afield. In the Val d'Orcia, a depopulated area in southern Tuscany, they found the 3,500 acre estate of La Foce. A forlorn desert of barren clay hills rising from a parched valley, the estate had been mismanaged for centuries; only a fraction of the land was good, only a fraction of that was cultivated, the forests were neglected and the twenty-five outlying farms were in varying states of disrepair – some were virtually inaccessible while most contained several dozen inhabitants crammed into a few dark, airless rooms. To the south stood the black, basalt cliffs and towering fortress of Radicofani, to the west was the summit of Monte Amiata, an extinct volcano which blocked the sea breezes but did nothing to stop the bitter tramontana wind from the north and the hot dry scirocco from the south.

Despite this unpromising prospect, the Origos were enchanted:

> To live in the shadow of that mysterious mountain, to arrest the erosion of those steep ridges, to turn this bare clay into wheat-fields, to rebuild these farms and see prosperity return to their inhabitants, to restore the greenness of these mutilated woods – that, we were sure, was the life that we wanted.

Following so soon after the devastation of the First World War, with its mustard gas, barbed wire and trench warfare, it is hardly surprising that the idealistic couple should decide to devote themselves to repairing the land. The estate had not always been barren, however, and Origo, a romantic as well as a budding historian, was as seduced by the region's past as by its potential future. In her autobiography she proudly recounts how the valley had been colonised by the Etruscans, how local chestnut woods had supplied timber for the Roman galleys in the second Punic war, and how, as part of the famous Via Francigena – the medieval pilgrim route to

LEFT *Atilla is said to have introduced the* maremmano *oxen from the Hungarian steppes to plough the heavy Italian soil; these picturesque creatures were loved by the Anglo-Florentines, as much for their noble patience as for their utilitarian strength. Gradually the* maremmano *were interbred with the* chianini, *finer white oxen from the Val di Chiana whom Origo described as 'gentle as evening moths'.*

ABOVE *Breaking with tradition, Origo filled the boxed edged parterres of her Fountain Garden with colourful flowers rather than the traditional coloured gravel or evergreen shrubs.*

Rome, the local roads had been linked to the whole of Christian Europe. In fact, her own villa had been built at the end of the fifteenth century as a hostel for those very pilgrims.

In the mid fifteenth century Pope Pius II, retreating to the region from the heat of Rome, extolled its verdant valleys, shady foothills and summits cloaked in beech woods: 'the ground is covered with fragrant herbs and wild strawberries, and among them small streams of clear water whisper their eternal song.' This rural idyll was destroyed a few decades later during the protracted wars between Siena and Florence. When the region was finally granted to Cosimo de' Medici, Grand Duke of Tuscany, the fighting had destroyed villages and devastated the land as peasants fled to the cities leaving fields untilled, forests unmanaged and slopes eroding to their dry, clay base. When the Origos arrived, four centuries later, the only hint of former glory was in the ruined battlements and towers littering the hilltops.

It is hard to imagine what would induce a shy, conscientious Englishwoman to leave the domesticity of Florence and settle in a bleak landscape three and a half hours journey from her family and friends. In her autobiography she admits to having felt uncomfortable amid the aimless, affluent expatriates. Perhaps this sense of drifting, compounded by her mixed heritage and cosmopolitan upbringing, drove her to put down roots, even in such alien soil.

As a writer, Origo was fascinated by the local peasants, noting their customs and superstitions, charting their lives in meticulous detail, particularly in the early days when the harvest was done by hand with long rows of reapers, binders and gleaners, bending low to the ground. Unusually, however, Origo could see beyond the picturesque scenes to empathise with the hardship involved in such a primitive lifestyle; after describing in sensuous detail the men naked to the waist, glistening with sweat, working the stone olive-press through the night by oil lamp, she notes, 'Now, in a white-tiled room, electric presses and separators do the same work in a tenth of the time….One can hardly deplore the change; yet it is perhaps at least worth while to record it.'

And record it she did, depicting the disappearing rural lifestyle in her autobiographical writings, celebrating the country's past in studies of the nineteenth-century poet Giacomo Leopardi, the fourteenth-century innkeeper's son turned politician Cola di Rienzo, the medieval Saint Bernardino, Byron's lover Countess Guiccioli, his daughter Allegra, several collections of biographical essays and *The Merchant of Prato*, a study of the medieval merchant, Francesco Datini.

Although writing provided intellectual stimulation, Origo's true passion was La Foce. Over the decades the Origos transformed the estate from a lunar landscape to a fertile valley of forests, wheat fields, olive groves, vineyards and reservoirs. By 1934 they had doubled the acreage and increased the number of farms from twenty-five

RIGHT *The luxurious garden was wrested from the corrugated, lunar landscape of* crete senesi – *clay hills, which Origo described as pale and inhuman, with 'the bleakness of the desert, and its fascination'.*

to fifty-seven. Even after the introduction of tractors however, the Origos initially retained the statuesque long-horned *maremmano* oxen, so beloved of the Anglo-Florentines, using these noble beasts to plough the steepest slopes.

While Origo concerned herself primarily with the garden, the couple operated as a team. Having purchased the estate with all of their combined capital they were dependent, for running costs, on her annual $5,000 income. Unlike many landowners the Origos were intimately involved in the workings of the farm; they were the first proprietors in a over a century to live on the grounds, the previous owners preferring to reside in Chianciano, the local spa town whose hot springs were fed by the underground fissures of the extinct Monte Amiata.

La Foce means 'the meeting point' as the fifteenth-century hostel was built at the intersection of the valley's two main roads. Although hardly the elegant villa Origo had pictured, over the years the pilgrim hostel had been transformed into a sturdy country house with a handsome three-arched ground floor loggia – a first-floor loggia above it having been filled in during the nineteenth century to create more interior space. While the Origos were on their honeymoon Cecil Pinsent was employed to install some basic comforts, adding a skylight to illuminate the central room, incorporating fireplaces, a bathroom, a library and sitting room.

Once the villa was habitable Pinsent moved on to oversee the restoration and expansion of the rest of the estate. As a lifelong bachelor he was easily absorbed into the family and after his friend and partner, Geoffrey Scott, married Lady Cutting, Pinsent would join the Origos at the Villa Medici for the family Christmas. In the early years of the Origos' marriage he travelled with them on several occasions and would reside at the villa for months at a time while engaged in design projects.

In larger estates like La Foce, a formal relationship prevailed between *contadini* and owner. Life centred on the *fattoria* or home farm. The psychological as well as the physical heart of the estate, the *fattoria* was where accounts were kept, decisions made and grievances aired. As well as housing the *fattore* or manager, his family and assistants, the *fattoria* contained the granaries and cellars for storing the owner's share of produce, the communal wine and olive presses, the laundry and woodsheds.

Unlike some grander villas, La Foce evolved with these utilitarian buildings attached to the main dwelling, spreading out around a central yard where the ox carts would unload the produce from outlying farms. Even after the need for protection had passed, many Tuscan villas retained this defensive layout to facilitate movement between buildings and enable the farm manager to oversee his staff. While the yard had to be kept open to receive the farm carts, Pinsent raised this functional space by transforming the large tank, used for laundry and watering livestock, into an elegant grotto-like pool. Over the years he was also to add a garage, clinic, school and community centre to the estate. In her autobiography Origo describes the bustle of the *fattoria*; the daily gathering for school, the weekly queue at the health clinic, the constant round of complaints and requests interspersed with seasonal rituals and religious rites as when the local priest and congregation would process through the field chanting litanies for fertility.

When Mussolini came to power in 1922 one of the ways he appealed to landowners was by promoting rural development with massive programmes of land drainage, road building and reafforestation. La Foce was part of a consortium of local landowners through which the Fascist government helped finance an eight bed clinic, a primary school and a kindergarten – for which Origo provided the novel luxury of a horse-drawn carriage to transport children from the most remote farms.

RIGHT *An old Tuscan saying, 'my grandfather's wood, my father's olive-grove and my own vineyard', describes how a barren hillside can be cultivated in three generations; Origo created her garden at La Foce in less than two decades.*

In later years Origo took pains to distance herself from the Fascists, but any large estate at the time had to make accommodations with the government, and its efforts at land improvement can only be applauded even if many of its other policies were deplorable. In any case, Origo was so integrated with the local community that she was spared the petty acts of xenophobia which might have alerted other expatriates to the growing antagonism towards the affluent nations of the west.

After expanding La Foce's *fattoria* and making the house habitable, Pinsent was asked to redesign the formal approach to the villa. The public road, which had passed right beside the villa's front façade, was diverted to create an elegant forecourt. This was screened from the new road with an imposing wrought-iron gate, whose double piers framed the front loggia. Origo promptly planted the short approach avenue with cypresses to give an imprimatur of age.

There was no garden at La Foce when the Origos arrived, just the remains of a *giardino inglese* which had probably been planted in the nineteenth century for ease of maintenance. In the early days water was scarce; the well barely provided enough drinking water and any excess went immediately to the farm. Soon after moving in, however, Origo began creating a small garden at the back of the villa, the furthest point from the busy *fattoria* courtyard. This was her private space, her bulwark against the vast, inhuman landscape. She later recalled how, on first viewing the property, she was overcome by a longing for gentle Florentine hills or green English fields – and most of all for a pretty house and garden to come home to. It was this that Pinsent helped her create.

Like I Tatti, Villa Medici and Le Balze, La Foce deviates from the Renaissance ideal in being sited, not at the crest of a hill, but halfway down the slope, with its main entrance perpendicular to the view. Rather than undertaking laborious landscaping, Origo and Pinsent worked with the topography, carving a garden from the slope itself. To further harmonise the garden with its setting they employed the rough travertine from a local quarry whose soft grey colour blends with the surrounding landscape. Although classical tradition demands sharp edges and clear detail, Origo favoured this rustic stone whose pitted surface retained earth, encouraging the growth of campanula, aubretia and alyssum to soften the lines of the architecture.

Soon after they purchased the estate Origo wrote to a former suitor explaining her vision of the future, which consisted of visiting the poor, running the school, playing the piano and writing books. Later, while pregnant with her first child, she reports she is planning both a nursery and a garden. Soon after, her letters reveal that despite the obligations of new motherhood, she is deeply engaged in the garden; thanking him for some rose bushes, she confesses that she spent the whole day planting them. Next she announces that the fountain is in place and she is going to pave the paths with travertine 'so that we should have at least one refuge on muddy days'. While a fountain might seem an extraordinary luxury in such a dry setting, water was an essential element of even the smallest Italian garden, animating the still, enclosed space and humidifying the air with its cooling splash.

However pleasing its effects, the fountain's trickle was sporadic until Origo's American grandmother, shocked to discover the privations under which the Origos

ABOVE *Nothing in her privileged upbringing prepared Origo for her role as chatelaine of La Foce where, despite being young and foreign, she was expected to dispense advice, help with illnesses and preside in the disputes of the peasant families. She found refuge from this bewildering responsibility in her garden, enclosed and separated from the bustle of the* fattoria *behind.*

were living, provided the funds to draw water from a stream six miles away. After adding new lavatories to the house, Origo turned, once more, to her garden, commissioning Pinsent to design a pergola to flank two sides of the space, backing the third side with a buttressing wall to support the slope behind, and enclosing the fourth with a stone wall whose tall entrance pillars frame the distant view of Monte Amiata.

Satisfied that there was enough water to keep the plants alive, Origo draped the pergola with purple wisteria and yellow banksia roses and filled the box parterres around the lawn with flowers. Against the slope she and Pinsent created an unusual laurel dome which they furnished with a stone bench so that Origo could attend to her correspondence on hot summer mornings while the children played on the grass nearby.

After the completion of the Fountain Garden in 1930, it was three years before Pinsent would work with Origo again, a hiatus caused, in part, because Origo's husband banished Pinsent after the chauffeur claimed he had seen his mistress cavorting with 'the engineer'. Although she was, at the time, having an affair with someone else, the accusation was not unfounded; many years later, when asked if she and Pinsent had been in love, she replied, 'Yes. I was and he was. But not at the same time.' While Origo had various romances, she might well have been Pinsent's main love; the gossipy annals of the community make no reference to his emotional engagements, yet he remained close to Origo to the end of his life. His temporary exile from La Foce was awkward, however, not least because he was restructuring the *fattoria* at the time, but evidently he managed to design from afar, as the work continued through his exile.

By 1933 the suspicion had passed and Pinsent was back in the garden where Origo commissioned him to push further into the landscape to create a Lemon Garden. This new space consisted of box-hedged enclosures containing large potted lemon trees on stone plinths. To protect the trees through the bitter winters Pinsent designed an elegant baroque *limonaia* beside the main gate. Facing this, across the front lawn, is a bronze sculpture of a mounted herdsman driving a herd of buffalo. This rustic pastoral scene was sculpted by Antonio's father, Marchese Clemente Origo, a cavalry officer who, having run off with the married mother of his illegitimate son, retreated to paint and sculpt in the obscurity of Florence.

In true English fashion, Origo smothered the walls of her Lemon Garden with roses, honeysuckle and jasmine while planting the edges with beds of peonies and lilies, both of which thrive in the heavy clay soil. This space was enclosed at the far end with a balustraded terrace overlooking the valley. Despite the Italian preference for eating indoors, Origo convinced her husband to dine here on summer evenings, and their daughter recalled how together they would stroll through the gardens talking over the events of the day then watching the sunset from the terrace.

When the Lemon Garden was complete, Origo and Pinsent created a Rose Garden, turning the buttressed slope above the villa into a long narrow terrace of geometric rose beds. This precarious plot is flanked by a magnificent wisteria-covered pergola which follows the curve of the hill to disappear around the corner. On the inner edge, Origo planted an herbaceous border in which she attempted to cultivate her favourite cottage flowers. Although lupins, phlox and delphiniums failed, imported English hollyhocks thrived in the hot Tuscan summers and the descendants of her first triumphs still flourish there today.

In 1933 when their eight year old son, Gianni, died of meningitis, Origo nearly abandoned the estate and the marriage: 'every inch of the house and garden, every field and tree, seemed full of his presence – I felt that I could not bear to come back.'

She did, however, choose to commit herself to La Foce, and asked Pinsent to design a family cemetery in which to lay her son.

Set into the hillside where it merges with the wider landscape, the cemetery is crowned by a stark, rectangular stone chapel whose sepulchral form is relieved by a simple Palladian porch. The terraced cemetery has family plots on the uppermost level, with the lower levels, in death as in life, reserved for staff and tenants. Although accessible from the main road, the cemetery is an integral part of La Foce to which it is linked by a grass path extending beyond the upper pergola. Like many before her, Origo found solace in horticulture and created a woodland garden around the cemetery. Combining wild herbs, flowering shrubs and ornamental trees she developed a serene, consoling, fragrant wilderness.

Through the 1930s Fascism had slowly infiltrated Italian life, imposing discipline on the people while promoting efficiency in industry, commerce and agriculture. Mussolini's wilder policies – forbidding the unhygienic handshake in favour of the clean Roman salute, promoting exercise, and insisting women wear feminine clothes – were a subject of mild amusement. His more oppressive measures, such as suppressing the press and rigging elections, went largely unnoticed in rural areas where newspapers were scarce and elections were often ignored anyway.

Even after Italy's invasion of Abyssinia in 1935, the support for Franco's Nationalists and the imposition of the anti-Semitic Race Manifesto of 1938, few acknowledged the links between the Fascists and the Nazis. In 1939 when Britain entered the war, the Anglo-Florentines refused to believe that Mussolini would join the fray. It was in this climate that Origo and Pinsent created the Lower Garden. A wedge-shaped space, accessed by an elegant double staircase from the Lemon Garden, this austere, flowerless, evergreen enclosure presents an image of humanist harmony in the face of contemporary chaos.

Divided into eight double-hedged 'rooms', the Lower Garden features an elegant grotto built into the staircase, and four magnificent *Magnolia grandiflora*. Although these glossy trees were not introduced from America until the eighteenth century, their conical forms harmonise with the garden's geometry and repeat the stone finials on the balustrades. A semicircle of cypresses screens the road beneath while providing a backdrop to a massive sculpture of a Caucasian carrying a sack of gardening tools. Beneath the sculpture a simple pool is backed by a curved stone bench which echoes a rustic bench at the base of the woodland slope above. Crowning the slope is a sculpture of a Moor carrying a cornucopia – a companion to the sculpture in the Lower Garden below. Contrasting the labour of the garden with the bounty of the wilderness, this subtle pairing underscores the dialogue played throughout La Foce between art and nature, as elements of the formal garden are echoed in the surrounding woodland.

BELOW Wisteria provides a leitmotif through the garden: this long wisteria-clad pergola winds round the slope of the hill, linking the formal garden with the wilder woodland beyond; another wisteria drapes the loggia which links the villa to the Fountain Garden, while a wisteria arbour in the forecourt shades an entrance to the villa linking the public space of the fattoria *with the private realm of the family.*

One of the key features of La Foce is located on a slope across the valley. Here, on a newly built road rising to a distant farm, the Origos planted a long, zigzaging cypress avenue. This archetypal scene has become one of the most photographed images in Tuscany; while providing shade to peasants on the road, the cypresses consciously recreate the landscape depicted in Benozzo Gozzoli's famous fresco in Florence's Medici chapel, created five centuries before.

In June 1940, soon after the Lower Garden was finished, Italy joined the war on the side of Nazi Germany. Pinsent returned to England to sign up with the Allies. Torn by divided loyalties, Origo went to Rome where, despite being an enemy alien, she was allowed to work for the Red Cross. Soon after, she gave birth to her first daughter, whom she sent back to the villa to be cared for while she continued her work in the city. Wartime in Rome was a catalogue of scarcity. In her account of the war years Origo recounts how a friend with six children had to sell twelve silver spoons to buy a small ham while elegant restaurants sprang up daily to provide excellent meals at exorbitant prices for the Fascist officials. Then she adds, soberly, 'It is generally expected that the harvest-fields will be destroyed by the Allies with incendiary bombs.'

Perplexed that the Italian people should turn against their natural allies and attempting, perhaps, to justify the betrayal of those among whom she had cast her lot, Origo explains that the Italians always felt the war had been forced upon them by the Germans, and in no sense did they feel responsible for their part in it.

In 1942, pregnant with her second daughter, Origo returned to La Foce. Compared with the privations of city life, the estate offered relative luxury, supplying both food and clothing with its own oil and wine, bread and meat, wood, wool, cheese and honey. Reverting to ancient practices, Origo made wooden clogs with leather tops from the tanned hide of the occasional calf, slaughtered in secret as government laws banned the killing of all but one pig per year. She also made her own soap with potato peelings, kitchen fat and soda. And when fuel was scarce she burned olive stones as her medieval forebears had done.

In 1944 the estate was deprived of meat, milk and eggs when a third of the cattle, 600 sheep and all the chickens and turkeys were killed or confiscated, first by the retreating Germans then by the incoming Goums – Moroccan units serving with the French army. In an act of particular malice the retreating Germans burned the bee-hives and took all the precious thread which Origo used to transform sheets, curtain linings, strips of felt and carpet into clothing for her own and the refugee children as well as the constant stream of fugitives passing through the estate.

Origo's diary of the war years, published as *War in Val d'Orcia*, is a poignant account of domestic routine alternating with terrifying risk. Fighting took place in fields near the villa while Origo herself assisted allies, deserters, Fascist soldiers and anti-Fascist partisans, feeding, clothing and sheltering them at various times and in various places about the estate. In 1943 La Foce was given a work party of English prisoners of war. After months of boredom at the POW camp, the prisoners were delighted at the prospect of agricultural work, thrilled with their clean rooms, the straw-filled sacks which served as mattresses and the rations which provided them with 400 grams of bread a day and meat twice a week – double what they had got at the camps. Origo also noted the huge Red Cross parcels which arrived for each prisoner every week containing tinned butter, marmalade, cocoa, potted meat, dried peas, bacon, cigarettes and a cake of excellent soap – 'bounty at which we all gape'.

In 1943 Origo transformed the villa's kindergarten into an orphanage to house twenty children evacuated from the city. After the war she continued to take in homeless, illegitimate, abandoned, tubercular, malnourished and convalescing children, attempting to find foster parents, first in America, then within Italy when Italian laws forbade the adoption of Italian children by foreigners.

After the intimacy and cooperation of the war years, the post-war period was a heart-breaking time of industrialisation and social agitation marked by redundancies, strikes and rural depopulation on a scale not seen since the Middle Ages. Adapting to the changing conditions, the Origos reorganised the farm, making use of machinery and depending less on manual labour. By 1970, of the fifty-seven farms, only six were still inhabited by their original tenants. Although a few had been taken over by skilled men who could manage the modern machinery, most were simply abandoned as tenants opted for an easier life of factory work or tourism in the nearby towns.

The gardens also had to adjust to post-war conditions. Like many of Italy's estates La Foce suffered accidental and deliberate damage during the war. When the villa was commandeered by the Germans, it was shelled by the Allies. By the end of the war the terraces were lined with machine gun trenches and pitted with shell holes, the lemon trees had been maliciously ripped from their pots and the land was littered with mines laid by retreating Germans. With post-war labour shortages the deep herbaceous borders could not be maintained, irrigation systems were installed and hedge clipping was reduced.

Like many of their countrymen the Origos considered selling in the 1950s when the threat of a Communist government was at its height. Having looked, unsuccessfully, for farms in England and America, they decided to take their chances and

ABOVE *An elegant tiered fountain animates the grotto inserted in the buttressing wall which separates the Lemon Garden from the Lower Garden below.*

remain. In the 1970s the Red Brigade posed a new danger with several local kidnappings attributed to the Sardinian shepherds who had settled the valley's abandoned farms. After their father's death in 1976 Origo's daughters attempted to sell the estate; when local workers unions objected, they divided the land, selling one third to a commune run by former estate workers. After several years of mismanagement that land was sold on to the cooperative of Sardinian shepherds which still owns it today. European Community subsidies have ensured that the valley has not completely reverted to sheep grazing, while the rise in rural tourism has allowed the abandoned farmhouses to be converted to holiday homes.

In 1988 Iris Origo died. Nine years later her daughter, Benedetta, opened the gardens at La Foce. Soon after, Caroline Moorehead's biography introduced the Marchesa to a new generation. Although a respected historian, many believe Origo's greatest legacy is her garden. The primary focus of her creative and emotional energy, it was a refuge from the harsh countryside, from the bustle of the farm, from the social life of the city and from the various tragedies of her life. It is also an autobiography in horticulture encoding the memory of an extraordinary woman and the people she loved. As one of the few grand gardens created in modern Italy, La Foce has immediate historical interest; while alluding to the past it also reflects the present with its unique blend of classical composition, Tuscan materials and modern simplicity. A twentieth-century pastoral in an ancient landscape, it demonstrates the best of the Anglo-Florentine tradition.

RIGHT *A framed view of the Lower Garden from the wooded hillside illustrates the intriguing interplay between civilisation and savagery, art and nature, the formal garden and the wild.*

DRAMATIS PERSONAE

Arthur Acton (1873–1953) Beaux-Arts trained artist turned art dealer, who, with his wife, Hortense Mitchell – of the Chicago banking family – purchased La Pietra, restoring the baroque villa, creating a noted garden around it.

Harold Acton (1904–1994) Arthur Acton's son; preserved and promoted La Pietra while writing books on Italian history.

Leon Battista Alberti (1404–1472) influential humanist architect, author of *The Ten Books on Architecture.*

Kinta Beevor (1911–1995) wrote vividly about growing up in the Anglo-Florentine community as the niece of Janet Ross and daughter of Lina Waterfield.

Bernard Berenson (1865–1959) American art historian; presided at I Tatti; initiated interest in early Tuscan Primitive painters.

Mary Berenson, nee Pearsall Smith (1864–1945) Berenson's Philadelphia-born wife; a Quaker of 'majestic proportions', an art historian in her own right who collaborated with Berenson on his early works and, with Cecil Pinsent, transformed the farmhouse of I Tatti into an elegant villa and garden.

Giovanni Boccaccio (1313–1375) Italian writer and humanist whose novel, *The Decameron* (c.1350) provided inspiration to the Anglo-Florentine garden makers.

William Merritt Chase (1849–1916) American Impressionist painter who visited Florence annually.

Henry and Esther Clifford owners of the Villa Capponi from the 1920s to the 1970s, when it was the centre of a sophisticated expatriate community. Henry Clifford was the curator of paintings at the Philadelphia Museum of Art.

James Fenimore Cooper (1789–1851) American writer, much influenced by his sojourn in Florence.

Earl (1847–1913) **and Countess** (1848–1939) **Crawford and Balcarres** late nineteenth-century owners of Il Palmieri.

Lady Sybil Cutting (1879–1943) Anglo-American bluestocking who restored the Villa Medici, renowned as the first humanist villa.

Harold Donaldson Eberlein (1875–1942) American architect; author of *Villas of Florence and Tuscany*, 1922.

Georgina Grahame early Anglo-Florentine who wrote of her horticultural efforts in her 1902 *In a Tuscan Garden*, followed in 1908 by *Under Petraia.*

Nathaniel Hawthorne (1804–1864) American novelist; spent the summer of 1857 in Florence as part of a sojourn in Italy with his family.

Sophia Peabody Hawthorne (1809–1871) Nathaniel's wife; published an account of her European travels in *Notes in England and Italy*, 1869.

Vernon Lee (1856–1935) pen name of Violet Paget; internationally renowned essayist who promoted the baroque style, especially as related to horticulture.

Joseph Lucas mysterious figure whose 1913 *Our Villa in Italy* lovingly describes creating a garden round his villa in San Domenico, north of Florence.

Mable Dodge Luhan (1879–1962) American heiress who, with her second husband, the Beaux-Arts trained architect, Edwin Dodge, restored the Villa Curonia before quitting the community and settling in Taos, New Mexico.

Nicky Mariano (1887–1968) Berenson's accommodating Italian secretary; inhabited I Tatti with the Berensons and remained after Mary's death as Berenson's companion.

Georgina Masson (1912–1980) pseudonym of Marion 'Babs' Johnson; garden historian whose 1961 *Italian Gardens* renewed interest in the subject after years of neglect brought on by the post-war taint of Fascism.

Michelozzo Michelozzi (1396–1472) favourite Medici architect; designed Villa Medici, Fiesole, in the mid-fifteenth century.

Henry Roderick Newman (1833–1918) American Pre-Raphaelite painter, settled in Florence in 1870.

Rose Standish Nichols (1872–1960) American garden writer and pioneering female garden designer; her 1928 *Italian Pleasure Gardens* fed interest in the subject.

Iris Origo (1902–1988) daughter of Sybil Cutting; with her Italian husband Antonio restored the 3,500 acre estate of La Foce and created a noted garden around its baroque villa.

Ouida (1839–1908) pseudonym of Maria Louise de la Ramée, an eccentric English novelist who settled in Florence, where *Friendship* her vicious 1878 *roman à clef*, exposed the Anglo-Florentine community as pretentious and greedy.

Walburga, Lady Paget (1839–1929) widowed wife of Augustus Paget, British ambassador, variously, to Florence, Rome, Copenhagen and Vienna; published eight volumes of diaries and letters, restored the medieval Torre de Bellosguardo.

Cecil Pinsent (1884–1963) influential British architect who designed for the Anglo-Florentine community, evolving a modern approach to villa gardens.

Charles Platt (1861–1933) American garden architect whose 1894 *Italian Gardens* was the first book in English on the subject.

Hiram Power (1805–1873) American sculptor; settled in Florence in 1837 and taught at the prestigious *Accademia*.

Janet Ross (1842–1927) prolific writer on Italian history, culture and cuisine; after serving briefly as Egyptian correspondent for *The Times* she settled outside Florence and farmed her medieval estate Poggio Gherardo.

Geoffrey Scott (1884–1929) British architectural critic whose influential 1914 *The Architecture of Humanism* helped revive the taste for baroque design.

Lady Scott daughter of the Duke of Portland; late nineteenth-century owner of Villa Capponi.

Sir George Sitwell (1860–1943) eccentric aristocrat whose 1909 *On The Making of Gardens* posthumously become a classic; restored the medieval Montegufoni.

Sir Osbert Sitwell (1892–1906) son of Sir George; preserved the estate and wrote amusingly about his father in various books.

William Blundell Spence (1814–1900) late nineteenth century owner of Villa Medici; painter and art dealer.

Sir Frederick Stibbert (1838–1906) eccentric collector; housed his sculpture in the parkland setting around his Villa Stibbert.

Charles Strong (1862–1940) American philosopher; commissioned Le Balze, first Italian villa designed by Pinsent.

Sir John Temple Leader (1810–1903) English MP who settled in Florence in the mid-nineteenth century; restored the ancient Villa Maiano, reconstructed the ruined castle of Vincigliata, reforested the hillside between them.

Frances Trollope (1780–1863) English-born writer who moved with her impecunious husband and seven children to America where her first book, *Domestic Manners of the Americans*, 1832, established her as a successful travel writer. In the 1840s she settled in Florence and became the centre of the expatriate community.

Mark Twain (1835–1910) pseudonym of Samuel Clements; American writer who lived in the Villa Viviani, Settignano in 1892, returning in 1903 to the Villa di Quarto with his ailing wife hoping the Tuscan air would cure her; it did not.

Lina Waterfield (1874–1964) Janet Ross' niece and ward; wrote on Italian politics and history. With her husband Aubrey Waterfield (1874–1944) she restored the medieval fortress of Aulla in Lunigiana where he created a 'sky garden' on the roof; moved to Poggio Gherardo after Ross' death.

Edith Wharton (1862–1937) American novelist and garden writer whose influential 1904 *Italian Villas and their Gardens* inspired a revival of interest in the subject.

Constance Fenimore Woolson (1840–1894) American novelist and friend of Henry James; known for her fictions about American expatriates in Europe.

Villas Open to the Public

(check opening times and days as these change frequently)

Le Balze
Via Vecchia Fiesolana 26, Fiesole, Florence; open by appointment; t: 055 59208; www.villalebalze.org

Torre di Bellosguardo
Via Roti Michelozzi 2, Bellosguardo, Florence; hotel; t: 055 229 8145; www.torrebellosguardo.com

Boboli Gardens
Piazza Pitti 1, Florence; open daily except the first and last Monday of each month, times vary with the season; t: 055 218 741 or 055 294 883; www.firenzemusei.it/00_english/boboli/index.html

Villa Capponi
Via Pian dei Giullari 3, Florence; open by appointment; t: 055 229 8609

Careggi
Viale Gaetano Pieraccini 17, Florence; government offices; open by appointment; t: 055 427 9755

Castello
Via di Castello 47, Castello, Florence; open daily except second and third Monday of each month; t: 055 454 791; www.polomuseale.firenze.it/english/musei/villacastello/

Villa Cetinale
Sovicille, Siena; open by appointment on weekday mornings; t: 0577 311147; cetinale@libro.it

La Foce
Strada della Vittoria 61, Chianciano Terme, Siena; open by appointment; t: 0578 69101; www.lafoce.com

Villa Gamberaia
Via del Rossellino 72, Settignano, Florence; gardens open daily, villa open by appointment; t: 055 697090; www.villagamberaia.com

Villa Maiano
Via Benedetto da Maiano 11, Florence; apartments; open by appointment; t: 055 599 600; www.fattoriadimaiano.com

Villa Medici
Via Beato Angelico 2, Fiesole, Florence; open by appointment; t: 055 59417

Montegufoni
Via Montegufoni 18, Montagnana, Florence; hotel; open by appointment; t: 0571 671 131; info@montegufoni.it; www.montegufoni.it/en/storia.html

Il Palmerino
Via Del Palmerino 10, Florence; apartments; open by appointment: t: 39 339 8444 725; www.palmerino.it

La Pietra
Via Bolognese 120, Florence; open by appointment; t: 055 500 7210; www.nyu.edu/lapietra/

Poggio a Caiano
Piazza de Medici 14, Florence; open daily except second and third Monday each month, times vary with the season; t: 055 877012; www.polomuseale.firenze.it/english/musei/poggiocaiano/

Villa Schifanoia
Via Boccaccio 121, San Domenico, Florence; European University; open by appointment; t: 055 46851

Villa Stibbert
Via Frederick Stibbert 26, Florence; museum; open daily except Thursdays; t: 055 475520; www.museostibbert.it/

I Tatti
Via di Vincigliata 26, Florence; open by appointment; t: 055 603 251; www.itatti.it

Vincigliata
Via di Vincigliata 21, Fiesole, Florence; hotel, by appointment; t: 055 599 556; www.castellodivincigliata.it/

BIBLIOGRAPHY

Acton, Harold, *Memoirs of an Aesthete*, Methuen, London, 1948

— *Tuscan Villas*, Thames & Hudson, London, 1973

Alberti, Leon Battista (trans. James Leoni), *The Ten Books on Architecture*, Alec Tiranti, London, 1955

Anon., 'An Italian Garden', *The Gardener's Chronicle*, 11 May 1912, p. 315

Anon., 'Le Balze', *Architectural Review*, LXXI, 1932, pp. 6–7

Beevor, Kinta, *A Tuscan Childhood*, Viking, London, 1993

Berenson, Bernard, *Sunset and Twilight*, Hamish Hamilton, London, 1964

Boccaccio, Giovanni (trans. G.H. McWilliam), *The Decameron*, Penguin, London, 1972

Bolton, Arthur T. (ed.), *The Gardens of Italy*, Country Life, London, 1919

Bowe, Patrick, 'I Tatti', *Country Life*, 5 July 1990, p. 90

Burckhardt, Jacob, *The Civilization of the Renaissance in Italy*, 1860, republished Phaidon, London, 1945

Cartwright, Julia, *Italian Gardens of the Renaissance*, Smith, Elder & Co., London, 1914

Ciacci, Margherita (ed.), *Of Queens' Gardens: The Myth of Florence in the Pre-Raphaelite Milieu and in American Culture,* Sillabe, Livorno, 2004

Coffin, David (ed.), *The First Dumbarton Oaks Colloquium on the History of Landscape Architecture: The Italian Garden,* Dumbarton Oaks, Washington, 1972

Dami, Luigi, *The Italian Garden*, Brentano's, New York, 1924

Eberlein, Harold Donaldson, *Villas of Florence and Tuscany*, J.B. Lippincott, Philadelphia and London, 1922

Elgood, George S., *Italian Gardens,* Longmans, Green & Co., London, 1907

Eubank, H., 'Poggio Gherardo', *The Gardener's Chronicle,* 3 December 1898, p. 397

Fantoni, Marcello, *Gli anglo-americani a Firenze,* Bulzoni, Rome, 1992

Fantoni, Marcello, Heidi Flores and John Pfordresher (eds), *Cecil Pinsent and his Gardens in Tuscany*, Edifir, Florence, 1996

Forster, E.M., *A Room with a View*, Knopf, New York, 1923

Graham, Georgina, *In a Tuscan Garden*, John Lane, The Bodley Head, London, 1902

Gunn, Peter, *Vernon Lee: Violet Paget,* Oxford University Press, London, 1964

Hill, May Brawley, *On Foreign Soil: American Gardeners Abroad*, Harry N. Abrams, New York, 2005

Hitchmough, Wendy, *Arts and Crafts Gardens*, V&A Publishing, London, 2005

Huxley, Aldous, *Those Barren Leaves*, Chatto & Windus, London, 1925

James, Henry, *Portrait of a Lady*, Macmillan, London, 1881

— *Italian Hours*, Houghton Mifflin, Boston and New York, 1909

Jones, Marchegiani Irene, and Thomas Haeussler (eds), *The Poetics of Place: Florence Imagined*, Leo S. Olschki Editore, Florence, 2001

Jullian, Philippe, and John Phillips, *Violet Trefusis: Life and Letters*, Hamish Hamilton, London, 1976

Latham, Charles, *The Gardens of Italy*, Country Life, London, 1905

Lazzaro, Claudia, *The Italian Renaissance Garden*, Yale University Press, New Haven and London, 1990

Leavitt, David, *Florence: A Delicate Case*, Bloomsbury, London, 2002

Le Blond, Mrs Aubrey, *The Old Gardens of Italy,* John Lane, London, 1912

Lee, Vernon, *Studies of the Eighteenth Century in Italy*, W. Satchell & Co., London 1880

— *Genius Loci*, John Lane, The Bodley Head, London, 1908

— *The Golden Keys*, John Lane, The Bodley Head, London, 1925

Lucas, Joseph, *Our Villa in Italy*, T. Fisher Unwin, London, 1913

Luhan, Mabel Dodge, *European Experiences*, Harcourt, Brace and Co., New York, 1935

Mariano, Nicky, *Forty Years with Berenson*, Hamish Hamilton, London, 1966

Masson, Georgina, *Italian Gardens*, Thames & Hudson, London, 1961

McCarthy, Mary, *The Stones of Florence,* Heinemann, London, 1959

Moorehead, Caroline, *Iris Origo: Marchesa of Val D'Orcia*, John Murray, London, 2000

Nichols, Rose Standish, *Italian Pleasure Gardens*, Dodd, Mead & Co., New York, 1928

Origo, Benedetta, Laurie Olin, John Dixon Hunt and Morna Livingston, *La Foce: A Garden and Landscape in Tuscany*, University of Pennsylvania Press, Philadelphia, 2001

Origo, Iris, *War in Val d'Orcia*, Jonathan Cape, London, 1947

— *Images and Shadows,* John Murray, London, 1970

Ouida, *Friendship*, Chatto & Windus, London, 1878

— *Pascarel*, Chatto & Windus, London, 1880

Paget, Lady Walburga, *Embassies of Other Days*, Hutchinson & Co., London, 1923

— *In My Tower*, Hutchinson & Co., London, 1924

— *The Linings of Life*, Hurst & Blackett, London, 1928

Pater, Walter, *The Renaissance*, Thomas B. Mosher, Portland Maine, 1902

Pemble, John, *The Mediterranean Passion*, Clarendon Press, Oxford, 1987

Pestelli, Andrea, *The Castle of Montegufoni*, Edizioni Il Fiorino, Florence, 2002

Platt, Charles, *Italian Gardens*, Harper & Brothers, New York, 1894, republished Timber Press, Portland, 1993

Ross, Janet, *Italian Sketches*, Kegan Paul & Co., London, 1887

— *Leaves From Our Tuscan Kitchen*, John Murray, London, 1899, republished 1973

— *Old Florence and Modern Tuscany*, J.M. Dent, London, 1904

— *Florentine Palaces and their Stories*, J.M. Dent, London, 1905

— *Lives of the Early Medici*, Chatto & Windus, London, 1910

Ruskin, John, *Sesame and Lilies*, George Allen, Orpington, Kent, 1887

Samuels, Ernest, *Bernard Berenson: The Making of a Connoisseur*, Harvard University Press, Cambridge, Massachusetts, 1979

Scott, Geoffrey, *The Architecture of Humanism*, Constable & Co., London 1914, republished Architectural Press, London, 1980

Secrest, Meryle, *Being Bernard Berenson*, Weidenfeld & Nicholson, London, 1980

Shacklock, Vincent, *Villa Le Balze*, Georgetown University, Florence, 1995

Shepherd, J. C., and Jellicoe, G. A., *Italian Gardens of the Renaissance,* Ernest Benn Ltd, London, 1925

Sica, Grazia Gobbi, *The Florentine Villa,* Routledge, Abingdon, 2007

Sitwell, George, *On the Making of Gardens*, Duckworth, London, 1909

Sitwell, Osbert, *Tales My Father Taught Me*, Hutchinson & Co., London, 1962

Sprigge, Sylvia, *Berenson: A Biography*, Allen & Unwin, London, 1960

Strachey, Barbara, and Jayne Samuels, *Mary Berenson: A Self Portrait from her Letters and Diaires*, Victor Gollancz, London, 1983

Treves, G. Artom (trans. Sylvia Sprigge), *The Golden Ring: The Anglo-Florentines 1847–1862*, Longmans, Green & Co., London, 1956

Vitruvius (trans. Morris Morgan), *The Ten Books on Architecture*, Harvard University Press, Cambridge, Massachusetts, 1914, republished Dover, New York, 1960

Von Arnim, Elizabeth, *Elizabeth and her German Garden*, Macmillan, London, 1898, republished Virago, London, 1986

Waugh, Evelyn, *Brideshead Revisited*, Chapman & Hall, London, 1945

Wharton, Edith, *Italian Villas and their Gardens*, The Century Co., New York, 1904

— *A Backward Glance*, D. Appleton, New York, 1934, republished Constable, London 1972

Whitsey, Fred, 'La Pietra', *Country Life,* 30 March 1978, p. 828

INDEX